Old Homes & Churches of Beaufort County, South Carolina

OLD HOMES & CHURCHES
of Beaufort County, South Carolina

BY MARY KENDALL HILTON

PHOTOGRAPHS BY ELLIS H. SKOLFIELD

Published by the State Printing Company
Columbia, South Carolina

PRODUCTION CREDITS

All Photographs were made with two 35MM Nikon FTN cameras fitted with a battery of eight (20 MM to 300 MM) Auto Nikkor lenses. The incomparable 35 MM PC-Nikkor was the primary lens. Dark room and original prints by E. M. Moore. Photo Lithography by Chromo-Lith. Photo composition in Garamond by Cold Type, Inc. Paper by Hopper is Ivory Sonata 80lb smooth, offset lithographed in two colors. The photographs by E. Skolfield of The State Printing Company are the property of the company and may not be reproduced in any manner without express written permission.

FIRST EDITION

LIBRARY OF CONGRESS NUMBER 72—137140
INTERNATIONAL STANDARD BOOK NUMBER 0—911432—17—5
MANUFACTURED IN THE UNITED STATES OF AMERICA

Designed By Ellis Skolfield

iv

This Book Is Affectionately Dedicated To My Husband, Ralph Hilton

PREFACE

The sweet smell of the resplendent magnolias, the sighing of tall pines, the gentle waving of scarves of Spanish moss in the warm trade winds, the dark waters of peaceful lagoons - all are joined in Beaufort County's tradition of beauty and langour. But it is a deceptive mask insofar as history is concerned. Three destructive wars, as a matter of record, have laid waste its fields and habitations. The fact that any of its old homes and churches survived is something to marvel at.

As far back as the early 1520's - when the Spaniards explored the area and gave it the name of Santa Elena - Europeans walked ashore in present day Beaufort County. The French Huguenot leader, Jean Ribaut, founded a colony at what he called Port Royal in 1562. The English colonial ship's captain, William Hilton, charted the waters around Hilton Head Island in 1663, and in 1670 William Sayle, governor of the colony arrived. In 1674 the Province of South Carolina was divided into four counties, Berkeley, Carteret, Craven, and Colleton, the latter encompassing what is now Beaufort County. The seat of government moved in 1679 to the present site of Charleston. An effort by fifty-one Scotch Covenanters in 1684 to establish a settlement, Stuart Town, on a bluff about a mile south of the present city of Beaufort ended in disaster August 17, 1686, when Spaniards from St. Augustine completely destroyed the village.

Beaufort County, which was formed in 1798, and the city of Beaufort were named after Henry Somerset, Duke of Beaufort. The frontier settlement, designated Beaufort Town in 1710, was repeatedly threatened in the prolonged hostilities with Spain, and was almost destroyed in the Indian conflict of the early 1700's. During the Revolutionary War the British, ranging between Charleston and Savannah, burned plantations and famous Sheldon Church. The town of Beaufort was spared during the War Between the States because the Northern Command wished to use its palatial homes and other buildings for hospitals and headquarters, and there today may be seen one of the South's most interesting assortment of surviving Low Country homes from the time of the indigo and rice and Sea Island cotton plantations dating back to the era of the Revolution, and even before. The years have not dealt so gently with the old churches although The Baptist Church of Beaufort and St. Helena's Episcopal Church in the city of Beaufort and The Church of the Cross in Bluffton still stand to impress and inspire us.

While even a brief visit to Beaufort can convey an idea of the profusion of historical treasures concentrated on one island, an explorer of the back roads of the county will come upon many rich rewards, for there are yet old churches and plantations left as reliquaries for the legends of our early hopes and dreams.

CONTENTS

ACKNOWLEDGEMENTS

I shall ever be indebted to the owners of Beaufort's old homes who received me most graciously, patiently answered my questions, and showed me their treasures. I found many friends among them and sensed the kindly presence of past owners long gone. I also wish to express my gratitude to the patient and always helpful staff of The Beaufort County Library and its branch on Hilton Head Island.

The histories of the homes and churches included in this book are hardly more than a sampling of Beaufort County's rich heritage, which is much too vast to fit into any one volume. I have made an earnest effort to sift the facts from legend and fiction, but am not sure that I have always succeeded for the records in some instances are scanty.

One of my problems was identifying the houses properly, for the names have been altered many times as ownership shifted throughout the years and designations have not always been made consistently. I sought guidance from the Office of Archeology and Historic Preservation of the United States Department of the Interior which referred me to *Recording Historic Buildings* by Harley J. McKee and I have applied the principles set forth in that work wherever possible and used the name of the original owner when it could be ascertained - "one which will continue to be meaningful regardless of changes in occupancy or use."

Mr. McKee further advised: "Hyphenated names should be sparingly used, and the ridiculous practice of adding another name to the chain every time the ownership of the structure changes is especially avoided. When a structure is widely known by a certain name, which may or may not be correctly applied to it, the common name deserves mention in parentheses."

Mary Kendall Hilton, Hilton Head Island, S. C.

The Historic Town of Beaufort

The Joseph F. Johnson House

411 Craven Street
Home of Mr. and Mrs. Howard Danner

The twilight of a lustrous era of fine plantation homes and town houses was settling over Beaufort, and the whole of the Low Country in the 1850's when Dr. Joseph F. Johnson, eminent planter and physician, decided to build a stately dwelling of his own in the town.

The house he constructed with the aid of an English architect stands majestically in the midst of a two-acre garden on The Point facing a great bend of the Beaufort River. Owned by Mr. and Mrs. Howard Danner, it is one of the few impressive ante bellum residences in the entire South that is still the home of a family connection of the original builder. Mr. Danner is a nephew of Porter Danner and Eliza Johnson Danner, Dr. Johnson's daughter, and he purchased the house from her heirs in 1944.

The house is also known as The Castle, a fitting description when it is viewed from Federal Street after the small marshy stream nearby has reached out a watery arm on a rising tide to create a moat. It has also been associated with the house which Francis Griswold designated as The Castle in *A Sea Island Lady*.

When Fort Beauregard fell and Federal troops approached in 1861 the Johnsons buried their prized china beneath the floor of a brick laundry adjacent to the house, loaded a few furnishings and other possessions into wagons and left hurriedly.

The house became a hospital with the laundry serving as a morgue. Ironically the bodies of the dead were to provide a macabre protection for the buried china, for it was recovered intact when Dr. Johnson redeemed his house after the war by establishing his claim and paying the taxes due.

Prior to its use as a hospital the house was a billet for troops. One evening while the soldiers were skylarking a member of the family return-

four

ed quietly across the river to the house. Under cover of the noise and confusion he gathered up a few small items and took them away in a skiff.

Some of these things have been returned to the house. A hurricane lamp chimney, survivor of the boat trip, sits in translucent calm upon a semicircular table - one of a pair - which is a returnee from the exodus by wagon. Two small stools, with rows of prim beading, do not betray even by a small scratch or stain their hazardous journey over the dark water.

A great sentinel oak, its girth now twenty feet, stands at the entrance to the house. With branches draped with tassels of Spanish moss it is part of the profusion of plantings which surround the house. Cedars, hollies, crape myrtle, palmettos, oleanders, and magnolias compete for dominance in a dramatic setting. The garden is spectacular in the spring when flowering shrubs and bulbs of many shades and varieties signal the start of a living color symphony that has few rivals in the private gardens of the Low Country.

Brick arches lift the house and enclose an English basement. Tall columns at the front carry the eyes upward, with the vertical sweep balanced by wide verandas with wooden balustrades on the second and third-story levels. A simple raised design of rhythmic curves flows along the top of the upper story.

The family pieces and other furniture of distinctive craftsmanship which Mrs. Johnson has assembled over the years are almost without exception from periods predating the construction of the house.

The living room atmosphere of charm and dignity is enhanced by a Chippendale chair back settee. A pair of gold and white Adam chairs flank the fireplace. The satin patina of a mahogany Sheraton chair harmonizes with delicate golden tones of an inlay in a mahogany desk from New England.

A wide center hall exemplifies the generous use of space throughout the house. At the back

twin stairways six-and-a-half feet wide lead to a large and airy landing which serves as an informal sitting room. Four bedrooms on this floor furnished with American and English antiques are large enough to accomodate tall highboys and four-poster beds with propriety.

The dining room to the right of the hall is furnished with an English table of mahogany with reeded legs. The chairs with feather adorned backs are of an authentic Charleston vintage coveted by collectors of Americana.

On the mantel of the dining room two Sevres vases provide a soft velvety blue background for the antics of a pair of cherubs. There is also displayed a notable collection of eighteenth-century silver from the fabled London workshop of the Bateman family.

Picturesque, history-suffused locales are an age-old breeding ground for ghosts. From the time of Dr. Johnson there have been reports of strange noises, mysterious door openings and closings, unexplained footprints, and the apparition of a stooped old man of dwarfish size, said by some to be Guenache, a French drummer with the Jean Ribaut expedition in 1562 who was hanged by a cruel captain. His ghost is reputed to have wandered over the marshes until Dr. Johnson's home, its appearance a nostalgic association with faraway Europe, offered shelter to the homeless phantom.

Mrs. Danner, herself, sets no store by wild tales of supernatural goings on, but she remarks casually with a smile that five generations who have lived in the house have seen and heard things which have not been explained satisfactorily.

For her part, she says that there are occasional door slammings, even when no wind stirs, that mystify the family. But neither she nor Mr. Danner have ever seen the ghostly Guenache.

315 Federal Street
Home of Mr. and Mrs. J. Riley Gettys

The policy of identifying Beaufort's old houses by the names of their original builders falters in this case, as the name of the builder cannot be ascertained. Something of his character and personality, however, may be deduced from the design of the house, with its honest, simple lines. He was, perhaps a straightforward man of somewhat Spartan taste. He chose slender squared posts for the verandas and severe wooden spindles to balustrade them. He must have been reasonably well-to-do, for he built a large white frame house rising two floors above a basement with spacious rooms divided upstairs and downstairs by a center hall. The only extravagant effect is contributed by nature in the richness of the green and tropical surroundings.

Built in the early 1800's the house was owned before the Civil War by John Bell, who married Margaret Bythewood. In 1863 after its owners had refugeed, it was acquired at a tax sale by one of John Bell's former slaves, Mary, for $500. She sold it later for $800 to Susie Bythewood Roberts, who had also been a slave.

The old house has survived the vicisitudes of the years to undergo a meticulous refurbishing and restoration in the hands of its present owners, Mr. and Mrs. J. Riley Gettys, who purchased it in 1965. (Mr. Gettys is president of Historic Beaufort Foundation, Inc.)

Harry Danner, Sr., father of Howard Danner who owns the Joseph Johnson House just around the corner, first rescued it from dissolution. The never-to-be-forgotten hurricane of 1893 had snatched the roof away and hurled one of its heavy timbers like a javelin through the walls of a building next door. Roofless beneath the subtropical sky for five years, the old house stood with its impermeable heart of pine floors and sturdy walls open to the weather. It is believed that during this period the original cornices and mantels were damaged or lost. One Adam mantel of ghesso survives in an upstairs bedroom.

When Mr. and Mrs. Gettys began the restoration of the old house they acquired Adam mantels and cornices, valuable relics of Beaufort's halcyon days and prime examples of the work of a master joiner, from a house then being demolished near the Baptist Church of Beaufort, providing ornamentation worthy of the splendidly dimensioned rooms. Mr. and Mrs. Gettys have furnished the house handsomely with antiques and family heirlooms.

Tidewater

The William Fripp House
302 Federal Street
Home of Mr. and Mrs. W. Brantley Harvey, Sr.

Enfolded in a mantle of timeless classic beauty, "Tidewater" overlooks the inland passage, thoroughfare of the Low Country from an ancient time when its aboriginal inhabitants traveled it in "canoas." William Fripp built the house around 1830 to accomodate his family in Beaufort when they made an annual summer visit from his plantation home on St. Helena's Island. He was a highly esteemed member of the Fripp family of planters and landowners who began to acquire land in the Port Royal area as early as 1695. An ancestor of his, John Fripp, was planting on St. Helena Island by 1725. By 1860 the Fripp family holdings had grown to more than twelve thousand acres, distributed among twenty plantations on adjoining islands. The Fripps practiced careful seed selection and cotton cultivation to produce the finest long staple Sea Island cotton. "Long cotton I make," is the way William Fripp expressed it in 1838 in a letter written to his relatives in Bristol, England. At the time of his death in 1860 he owned more than three thousand acres of land on St. Helena Island valued at twenty-five dollars an acre and was one of the wealthy men of his day.

When the rebuilding of the Baptist Church of Beaufort was begun in 1842 he made a large contribution. His friends and neighbors spoke of him as "Good Billy" or "Righteous Billy." During the Civil War his wife, Sarah, and their children fled to Aiken, South Carolina, never to return to Beaufort. The Federal government confiscated the house and held it until 1867.

A story was current for many years that this house had been cut in half and transported by barge to its present site from Lady's Island and that upon arrival it was reassembled upside down. Mr. and Mrs. Harvey, who bought it in

1936 had this theory checked out by a team of engineers and architects. After careful study the experts stated that, although this was a highly intriguing notion, it simply could not be true for many reasons, including the fact that the stairwell would not have fit had the floors been reversed. The ceilings of the upper story are six inches higher than those of the lower. It has also been observed that the doorway to the upper piazza has a decorative fanlight with sidelights whereas the lower doorway, also with its sidelights, is crowned with simple rectangular panes. However, the view of the facade of the stately white house from the water's edge is one of harmony and perfect proportions. The upper door, framed by two of the four columns of the piazza, is flanked by engaged columns as is the door below. A more extensive use of moldings around the lower door gives it emphasis and dominance, proper for the main entrance to the house.

Mrs. Harvey has called her home by the romantic name of "Tidewater" and has filled it with furnishings and appointments of formality, many of them older than the house itself, such as a mahogany Chippendale bureau bookcase

dated 1770 in the drawing room, a pair of 1790 fruitwood chairs with their original needlepoint covers, and two eighteenth century Chippendale "stuff-over" chairs with reeded mahogany legs. These chairs are covered with pale green damask to match the color of the walls and the curtains at the tall windows, which are artfully hung within the window framing so that the admirable moldings are not obscured. Adjacent is a sitting room with a mellow antique desk of early American vintage. Across a center hall, flooded with light from a very large window on the landing and the controversial fanlighted door, is the dining room. The dining room has an old Sheraton sideboard laden with English silver, a chest of drawers which has been in the Harvey family for many years, and a quaint corner cupboard with an inlay of holly wood which was brought from the mountains of North Carolina.

"Good Billy's" slave artisans were skilled workers though they did perhaps make an error in the measurement of the upper story. The wooden mantels - identical throughout the house - are elaborately carved interpretations of the Greek Revival theme. They also produced a fine Adam stairway of mahogany and walnut with lovely slim spindles. Even the face boards of the stringers of the stairway are adorned with stylized carved designs. The half-rounded designs of the moldings of the plaster cornices and wooden door and window moldings are of varying widths and depths to provide undulating surfaces for a lovely and interesting interplay of light and shadow.

While preserving one of Beaufort's most distinguished old homes, Mr. and Mrs. Harvey have assembled letters and papers to document its history including copies of William Fripp's letters and his will, correspondence with his descendants, and a letter from Robert Woodward Barnwell describing happy childhood days frolicking in the tree shaded environs of "Tidewater" overlooking the historic waterway.

The Edward Means House
604 Pinckney Street
Home of Mr. and Mrs. Chester White, Sr.

Surrounded by a walled garden spangled with glossy magnolias and luxuriant with flowering shrubs, the Edward Means House is built of brick in shades of coral and vermillion complemented by white woodwork. It combines the use of the finest materials and workmanship and is an outstanding example of a period, called by Lena Wood Lengnick in *Beaufort Memoirs*, the "splendid fifties." The well-pointed brickwork was done by Franklin Talbird. This was one of many houses in Beaufort preserved from destruction during the occupation because of the Federal needs for quarters and hospitals for Union soldiers.

Colonel Edward Means bought the lot in 1853 and built the house shortly thereafter. In 1871 he sold it to Henry M. Stuart who operated one of the first Eli Whitney cotton gins at Port Republic and West Streets a few blocks away. In 1968 Mr. and Mrs. Chester White, Sr.

purchased it from Mr. and Mrs. George Tucker who had made it their home for many years.

Semicircular steps lead to a curved portico at the entrance on the east. Inside the house a hall opens into an ample stair hall with a spectacular flowing staircase which is partly freestanding.

The design of the rooms is a departure from the customary Low Country center hall plan. The hall extends almost the length of the house with two drawing rooms and a dining room on the left facing toward the south. Wide verandas receive cooling breezes in summer and sunshine in winter. (The floor plan is similar to some of the houses on the Battery in Charleston.) The drawing rooms and the dining room are connected by wide doorways framed by handsome moldings and cornices. Sliding doors permit the rooms to be opened up as one. In this magnificent expanse of space crystal chandeliers sparkle above sculptured white mantels and the patina of polished rosewood, mahogany, and walnut furniture. A rich accent is provided by the gleam of a gold-framed mirror hung above a Victorian table with a white marble top. The sideboard and table in the dining room are of walnut deeply carved in a rope design.

Mr. and Mrs. White are acquiring the work of regional painters to bring Sea Island landscapes and seascapes indoors. The master bedroom on the second floor has a Chippendale mahogany tester bed, circa 1770, with carved posts and a canopy of linen in a Chinese design.

eleven

Marshlands

The James Robert Verdier House
501 Pinckney Street
Home of Mr. and Mrs. Sterling Harris

Marshlands has acquired a rich history since the start of its construction in 1810, and encloses within its walls the shadows of a widely varied collection of characters, many of whom never lived at all except in the realm of imagination.

The name "Marshlands" was given to the house by Francis Griswold who set his novel, *A Sea Island Lady,* in the Civil War period and its aftermath with a focus on an impressive Beaufort home which he called Marshlands - (locally still identified as the old James Robert Verdier house) - utilizing composite features from several other historic Beaufort homes.

The novel was published in 1931, and for more than a quarter of a century visitors have been entering the hospitable gates of Marshlands to stroll the grounds where the fictional Fenwick family rose to wealth and power and were engulfed by the Yankee invasion. Inside the house they look about as if to catch a glimpse of star-crossed Emily Easton Moffet, Stephen Fenwick's beloved beauty from the North; or of carpetbaggers or the cigar smoking correspondents from the New York Newspapers. Or, General Sherman himself.

And on the way out there is usually a last, long turn around the lawn to hear, perhaps, the voice of Alec, the Fenwick's slave boy: "De debble mus' be 'pontop you' tail!"

Marshlands was built by Dr. James Robert Verdier, who achieved prominence in the practive of medicine, and was renowned for his success in treating yellow fever patients.

The home was lost to the Verdier family either during the War Between the States or in the critical years preceding the struggle. In brooding isolation behind a high planked wall and wooden gates topped with an official sign, "U. S. Sanitary Commission," Marshlands

endured the war years 1861-1865 and outlived the occupation. During the years of Reconstruction and until 1940, it was owned at different times by several families from various sections of the United States.

In 1940 the house was acquired by Mr. and Mrs. Sterling Harris who came down from Maryland to make their home in Beaufort. A cultivated couple with an appreciation of America's architectural heritage and a love of antiques, they entered upon a carefully planned restoration that was to require years for completion.

An airy piazza in the style of the West Indies across the front and along two sides of the house provides shade and coolness. The entrance hall, drawing room, dining room, and library with twelve-foot ceilings and tall windows for cross ventilation are proportioned for comfort in semitropical heat.

As the visitor crosses the veranda and enters the wide hall of Marshlands the first impression is one of balance and noble proportions. The stairway is well to the rear of the hallway back of an arch with fanlight. The hall is furnished with many fine pieces including an inlaid mahogany card table with a folding top over which hangs an original Chippendale mirror. A desk from Pennsylvania dating from 1790 which came from Mrs. Harris' family glistens with Sandwich glass drawer pulls in pristine condition.

To the right of the hall is the drawing room with a splendid Adam Mantel. Garlands and delicate traceries surround a classic Roman head characteristic of the style. Outstanding in this room is the authentic Louis XV commode. A lamp of Meissen china from two centuries ago sheds a glow over the elaborate inlay of the commode illuminating at the same time its own motif of roses and raised sprays of pink and blue forget-me-nots.

The mantel in the dining room, which is to the left of the hall rivals the one in the drawing

English wallpaper in a delicate pastoral design of soft, glowing colors. Another four-poster of equal impressiveness is in the bedroom across the hall.

Marshlands, shaken by an earthquake in 1886, buffeted by the winds of many hurricanes, beset by wars and the victim of a mysterious fire in recent years, is now carefully restored and furnished with taste and distinction by owners who are sensitive to the demands which an old house can impose, and appreciative of the rewards which it can bestow.

room in charm and has an added element of mystery. The dominant figure of a nymph is minus its head. An incident in *A Sea Island Lady* describes how a Union soldier during the Civil War pried an ornament from a mantel at Marshlands with a bayonet. Mrs. Harris, sympathetic to the romantic interests of her visitors, has left this detail unrestored.

The mahogany dining room chairs belonged to John Eager Howard of Maryland - an ancestor of Mr. Harris - notable for his exploits during the Revolution and for a later dis-

tinguished career as governor of Maryland. They are eighteenth-century American Hepplewhite. The three-part Hepplewhite table, also of mahogany, is distinguished by an exquisite inlay in a husk motif. Inlaid oval medallions adorn the bow-front mahogany sideboard.

On the second floor the furniture is also in the museum piece category. A 1780 cherry field bed, flanked by tall windows stands in Mrs. Harris' bedroom. A mahogany chest of drawers with its original Sandwich glass knobs is ranged against a wall covered with imported

The John Chaplin House

712 New Street
Home of Mrs. Chlotilde Martin

The Chaplin family came early to the wilderness of South Carolina as pioneering homesteaders. The first John Chaplin and his wife, Phoebe Jenkins, settled on Edisto Island in 1675 and later moved to St. Helena's Island. The Chaplins are listed among the planters on St. Helena as early as 1725 and the first census of the infant republic records that in 1790 another John Chaplin owned thirty slaves. He was the eldest son of John F. Chaplin and shortly after the taking of the census he built the simple colonial house which still stands today.

The original house was a story and a half high with two rooms downstairs and an enclosed stairway leading to two bedrooms with dormer windows tucked under a sloping roof. It has undergone minor changes and additions but retains an old fashioned down-to-earth personality. Built of heart of pine put together with pegs, it has paneled doors and wainscoting, and exhibits as a hallmark of its antiquity the signs of the adz and plane left by long dead craftsmen. The chimney of hand made brick on the east or New Street side is not attached to the wall of the building. It stands free a good ten inches away, an early practice to prevent fires. The design can be seen in other old Beaufort houses as well as in buildings in Maryland and Virginia.

sixteen

The Oaks

The Paul Hamilton House
100 Laurens Street
Home of Mr. and Mrs. Paul Schwartz

Secluded in a bower of august oak trees with limbs so heavy that many of them touch the ground, the Paul Hamilton House is located on The Point overlooking the marshy reaches of the Beaufort River. Azaleas, camellias, and oleanders provide varying shades of green for the grounds of the old white house, an edifice built in 1856 by Colonel Paul Hamilton, whose grandfather Paul Hamilton, Secretary of the Navy from 1808 until 1812, in President James Madison's Cabinet, had served in the Revolution at the age of sixteen, later becoming a planter of indigo and rice and holder of many public offices in South Carolina including that of governor.

Slightly lifted on brick foundations with broad upper and lower verandas on three sides, the house has beautifully executed exterior and interior woodwork. The bed molding of the cornice beneath the overhang of the roof has spade-shaped wooden blocks in a variation of the denticulation frequently seen in Adam-inspired architecture. The wider molding which completes the design has modillions terminating in carved wooden finials. This same inverted urn motif is also used in the modillions of heavy cornices incorporated into the lintels over the doorways and windows.

The core of the house is its wide, sunlet center hall with paneled wainscoting and a stairway with hand carved spindles and an unusual and interesting newel post composed of flourishing curlicues. The drawing room to the right and the dining room on the left display Adam mantels and woodwork of classic simplicity.

The Hamilton family fled after the Battle of Port Royal and the defeat of the Confederate forces. They returned to Beaufort five years later in November of 1866, According to Mary

S. Hamilton, Colonel Hamilton's daughter, they arrived "in a large four-horse wagon . . . (drawn by mules) 'packed like sardines,' and in spite of all happy to see once more the salt water of our dear old home . . ."

"The Oaks" had been used as a hospital during the War and the Government Commissioners were offering it for sale along with many other houses in Beaufort "for taxes due." Colonel Hamilton hurried off to Charleston to sell property there in order to raise the money to redeem his home. He had been allowed only three days to accomplish this. The story continues in Mary Hamilton's own words: "The day before my father could possibly return, two Northerners heard that the Commissioner intended to sell the house at private sale, after sunset, unless the money was paid before. They collected the required amount, at their own risk, and one of them went to the commissioner and paid it down just before the time was up. As he was leaving the office, the sun set, and the man who expected to purchase entered, so that he heard the commissioner say: 'You are too late, the money has been paid.' We shook hands with the Northerner that night, though up to that time we had said would never give a handshake to any Yankee." (Lena Wood Lengnick in *Beaufort Memoirs* identifies the Northerners as, "a Mr. Simpson and Mr. George Holmes." George Holmes bought the George Parsons Elliott House for taxes after the war.)

Colonel Hamilton's contemporaries admired the quality of the materials he used and the care he exercised in the building of his home. The timber was cut on his island plantation, well seasoned, and carefully selected. For sixty years it required no repairs, it is said, except on one occasion when a storm blew the roof off in 1896. Mr. and Mrs. Paul Schwartz, the present owners, have given the house meticulous care and it has been preserved like a fine jewel in a rare and beautiful setting.

Bevers Barnwell Sams House, (II)

201 Laurens Street
Home of Mr. and Mrs. E. G. Herendeen

This noble house in fluid Regency style was built in 1852 by Dr. Bevers Barnwell Sams and is considered one of the best examples of that style in the Beaufort area. Constructed of varitoned bricks and dappled by the shade of surrounding trees, it has four Doric columns across the front supporting upper and lower piazzas. The bulk of the columns is countered

by wooden balustrades of a fragile, lacy design. A wooden parapet in the same airy pattern surrounds the flat roof. The combination produces a balanced and singularly pleasing effect. A photograph taken during the Civil War when it was Federal Hospital No. 8 shows the house without the parapet and with plain railings on the upper veranda.

Dr. Sams was the younger brother of Lewis Reeve Sams who built the commanding town house at 601 Bay Street. He owned half of Datha Island with his brother. The tabby ruins of the family's plantation homes and a chapel, all destroyed by forest fires, may still be seen on Datha Island. Previously Dr. Sams had built a house at 310 New Street in Beaufort. He died in 1855 only three years after building his fine new home on Laurens Street.

In 1896 George Crofut bought the property. Since that time it has been continuously occupied by his descendants and is frequently referred to as The Crofut House. Mr. and Mrs. E. G. Herendeen are the present owners. It is one of the houses frequently opened to the public during the spring tours sponsored each year by the Churchwomen of St. Helena's Episcopal Church. Amid a display of spring blossoms visitors have an opportunity to trace the pattern of an old formal garden at the side of the house and explore one of Beaufort's most picturesque ties with the past.

The furnishings of the parlor to the right of the center hall include fine Victorian sofas and chairs of rosewood inlaid with mother-of-pearl and cane-bottomed French and Italian chairs. In the music room to the rear of the parlor there are portraits of George Crofut and his wife painted by Nahum Ball Onthank. The house has several fine marble mantels.

A picturesque tabby building is preserved behind the house. Its rooms were originally used for a kitchen, a carriage house and quarters for house servants.

The Hugh Hext House
207 Hancock Street
Home of Mr. and Mrs. Ridgeway Hall

Hugh Hext, who arrived from Dorchester, England, in 1686, was one of the courageous pioneers of the Port Royal demesne. By the time Beaufort was christened in 1710 he had obtained a warrant for land on St. Helena's Island, although the Spaniards had not yet conceded that it was English territory. A few years later, around 1725, he built a summer house on what is now known as The Point in Beaufort. In those days it was called Black's Point and Hugh Hext owned the little peninsula, which was out in the country. Not until the early nineteenth century did Beaufort extend its city limits to the east naming the streets to honor statesmen of the new republic. One of his descendents, Elizabeth Hext, who inherited the house, married William Sams, grandson of "Tuscorara Jack" Barnwell. Eventually so many members of the Sams family owned houses on The Point that for a time it was called Sams Point.

Restoration of the house, which broods over the marshes and the Beaufort River, with Lady's Island in the distance, has been completed by Mr. and Mrs. Ridgeway Hall who purchased it in 1968. Set off by a low brick lacework wall the spacious house rises two stories above a high pink basement. Twin verandas are enclosed by neat spindled balustrades.

The renovation of the house was first begun some twenty years ago by Mrs. Irma Morris of Pickens, South Carolina, who had an antique shop there. To her delight and surprise she found that the linoleum which covered the floors concealed the original pine board flooring. When she removed paint and flimsy partitions old paneling and wainscoting were revealed.

The late Miss Mabel Runnette, librarian of

the Beaufort County Library for many years, pictured the furnishings of a house such as this in *Early Settlement of Beaufort Town - 1700 - 1725*: "Furniture for these homes had either to be brought from England or made on the plantation by the slaves. Silver and pewter likewise must be imported for no pewter was made in the colonies until after 1732. Fingers were more fashionable then than now for there were few table forks and knives were useful for many purposes. Fireplace cooking prevailed, with the huge pots and long handled skillets of the day: clothing was made at home by way of the spinning wheel and loom; wigs there were for the gentlemen and curls for the ladies, elaborate dresses, full skirted, trailing the ground, tight laced bodices with many frills, long full skirted coats and knee breeches for the men with silver buttons and silver buckles at the knee and on the shoes."

Mr. and Mrs. Hall have completed the restoration begun by Mrs. Morris and filled the house with their inherited collection of New England antiques. Happily a very important old house, one of the oldest in Beaufort County, is returned to its former splendor.

The John A. Johnson House

804 Pinckney Street
Home of Mr. and Mrs. Milton Parker, III

A room-by-room plan of restoration which will require several years to complete has been started to reclaim a deserving old Beaufort house after years of neglect and decay and return it to its former status of a pampered home. When Mr. and Mrs. Milton Parker, III, bought the Joseph A. Johnson House three years ago it had been cut up into ten apartments with kitchenettes and baths intruding onto verandas designed over a century ago for a more gracious usage.

The house was built in the early 1850's by Dr. John A. Johnson. His wife was Claudia Talbird, sister of Franklin Talbird who did the construction work. Franklin Talbird also built the Edward Means House on Pinckney Street two blocks away.

The old Johnson home, featuring white painted brick, is similar in floor plan to the Edward Means House, although designed on a smaller scale, with a hall leading to a stairway with two drawing rooms on the left and beyond these a dining room. The Johnson house has white columned porticos on three sides. White marble entrance steps bracketed with iron railings lead to a small landing with a rectangular canopy supported by carved wooden modillions. The drawing room at the front of the house has a black marble mantel unadorned except for the graining pattern of the marble on the chimney breast. The two adjoining rooms have deal mantels painted white.

Dr. Johnson, described by one of his contemporaries as a "man of learning and individuality," wrote his remniscences, *Beaufort and the Sea Islands, Their History and Traditions,* in a series of articles which appeared in *The Beaufort Republican* in 1873. He told of Beaufort's history, its people and its institutions and promised his readers "a faithful record of those

incidents and events 'all of which I saw, and part of which I was' ". His narrative, a useful reference for historians, is preserved in the Beaufort County Library.

Mr. and Mrs. Parker have furnished the restored portion of the house with furniture of several periods including French pieces. Interesting accents are a twelve-branched ormulu chandelier which still burns candles and an old Chinese screen with beautiful coloring.

three separate houses. In the New Street house Mrs. Sams has preserved pictures of the old house, chapel and burying ground along with a wealth of portraits, photographs, and other family memorabilia.

One aspect of plantation life on Datha has been preserved for us through the writings of the Reverend George W. Moore, a Methodist minister who went there on an evangelistic mission to the Gullah slaves in 1832. He preached week days and Sundays in Beaufort and on its circumjacent islands. At some places he preached at night with a Negro illuminating the pages of his hymnbook and Bible with a lightwood torch. Dr. Sams, as did the majority of the planters, supported the mission, bringing his slaves in from the fields to hear the words of the minister.

The Thomas Hepworth House
214 New Street
Home of Mr. and Mrs. Somers Pringle

Her most Serene and most Sacred Majesty Queen Anne was England's ruler when the Lords Proprietors agreed together in 1710 that a seaport town would "be erected in Port Royal in Granville County in South Carolina, to be called Beaufort Town" in honor of the Duke of Beaufort. The town was actually laid out in 1717 during the reign of King George I and one of the first lots on the southwest corner of New and Port Royal (now Port Republic) Streets was granted to Chief Justice Thomas Hepworth of Charleston August 10 of that year under the order passed by the council of the Province "that every person who took up any of the front lots should be obliged to build thereon a house of fifteen feet in breadth and thirty feet in length in two years time." Owners of back lots were allowed an additional year to build. Although the order was not always rigidly enforced, it is not unreasonble to assume that the small white clapboard Colonial house

The Bevers Barnwell Sams House (I)
310 New Street
Home of Mr. and Mrs. Arthur Raoul Sams

This forthright old house has maintained a firm stance at 310 New Street ever since Dr. Bevers Barnwell Sams built it in 1818 (or completed a house already under construction on the site begun by the Cuthbert family.) There probably *was* an earlier building there as the lot had been granted to William de Veaux in 1764. Dr. Sams' son, Melvin Melius, inherited the property in 1855. Except for an interval during the Civil War when it was confiscated and used as Federal Hospital No. 10 for contrabands, former slaves under the jurisdiction of the Union forces and treated as contraband of war, it has been owned and occupied by lineal descendants of Dr. Sams. Its present occupants,

Mr. and Mrs. Arthur Raoul Sams represent the fourth generation.

The house conforms to the pattern of a Low Country house of the period, built on a high foundation with two large verandas facing south. It originally had six rooms on three levels with kitchen, servants' quarters and stables apart. Additions have been made to the house by succeeding generations of the Sams family.

The progenitor of the Sams family, Bonham Sams, left his native England to take his chances in the wilds of the New World in 1681. His grandson, William, husband of Elizabeth Hext, bought 12,000-acre Datha Island in 1783. Upon William Sams' death in 1798 his sons, Bevers Barnwell and Lewis Reeve, shared the inheritance of Datha. Dr. Sams added wings on each side of the old family home there, creating still standing today and considered by many to be the oldest house in Beaufort, was built around 1722 by Chief Justice Hepworth.

The stated purpose of the order was "to forward the speedy settlement of the said town of Beaufort to the strengthening of the frontiers of the Province against all manner of enemies." Nevertheless, James Sutherland, an English- man who passed that way in the late 1720's found, "but few Stragling houses meanly in- habited, which on the contrary ought always to have a great many men to prevent Pyrates destroying the country . . . The people being afraid to settle . . . so near the Spaniards of St. Augustin's who are continually encouraging the Indians to destroy them." The Thomas Hepworth house was built as a stronghold as well as a dwelling with thick tabby foundations pierced by long slits to facilitate the aiming and firing of muskets. In 1741 the property was purchased by Thomas Burton from Thomas Hepworth for eighty pounds.

Dr. Archibald Johnson, writing in 1873 in *Beaufort and the Sea Islands,* refers to the

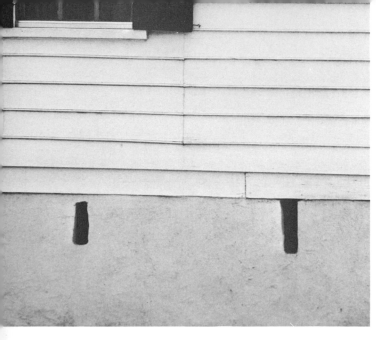

house as an "antiquated, Dutch-looking building." He also relates some of the happenings there during the Revolution as told him by Mrs. Rebecca Johnson, his grandmother, who lived there then and as a very old lady remembered the day a cannon ball shot from a British warship anchored in the Beaufort River passed over her head and through her house to strike down a horse grazing several hundred yards away. Mrs. Johnson also recalled that the same British General Augustine Prevost, whose troops were responsible for the first burning of Sheldon Church, disciplined some of his men by putting them in irons because they attempted to make off with her silver plate.

Some time after Mrs. Johnson's unsettling experiences, at the close of the eighteenth century, the first single-roller cotton gin was set up and exhibited in the front parlor of the house. It was used by William Fickling as a school for boys, served as a Masonic Lodge, and passed through many hands until Mr. and Mrs. Pringle acquired it from Miss Mary Waterhouse in the 1950's.

The story-and-a-half house has been enlarged by partially or entirely closing porches but the lines of the original construction with a gable and dormer windows remain almost

intact. The large living room, entered to the left of a front porch is wainscoted and runs the depth of the house. The dining room now contains a corner cupboard which was moved from the kitchen because of its intriguing similarity to one in the House of the Seven Gables in Salem, Massachusetts. An enclosed stairway leads from the living room to two bedrooms and a bath on the second floor where the ceilings follow the varying lines of the roof. One of the bedrooms is furnished with antiques from the estate of Charles Carroll of Carrollton, Maryland, patriot leader, delegate to the Constitutional Convention in 1776, and a signer of the Declaration of Independence who had the distinction of outliving all of the other signers. (He died in 1832.) A brick-walled old fashioned garden rounds out the charm of the scene.

The George Mosse Stoney House
500 Port Republic Street
Home of Mr. and Mrs. Roscoe Mitchell

One of Beaufort's early-day home builders chose for himself a magnificent water-oriented view and erected a residence which came to be immortalized in the John Campbell picture of old Beaufort of 1799 which hangs in the Beaufort County Library.

Some fifty years later Dr. George Mosse Stoney, son of Dr. John Stoney who came to America from Scotland in 1774, acquired the house and its scenic environs overlooking the Beaufort River. He enlarged it and made many changes, adding wide upper and lower verandas on three sides, and lofty grooved columns to achieve the imposing mien of the house as it appears today.

Sedate denticulated trim on the roofline varies from that frequently found in houses of the era. The "teeth" are very slender and set farther apart. The entrance steps are of brick with white spindled wooden bannisters. Open brickwork screens the foundation of the house.

To the right of the entrance there is a brick terrace rimmed with fragrant stock, willowy blue sage, snap dragons, and other colorful blossoms thriving in the Low Country's long growing season.

The woodwork of the wainscoting, and the door and window moldings of the drawing room and dining room, separated by a hallway, are painted a soft shade of blue turquoise to contrast with the white plaster of the walls. The wide window and door moldings have deep groovings and a design of squares within a larger square at the top corners. Damask draperies falling from matching valances are hung within the window moldings so that the carving is visible.

The chatelaine of the house, Mrs. Roscoe Mitchell, is the great-granddaughter of Gustav Pollitzer, an Austrian jeweller who was the first of the five generations of the Pollitzer family who have occupied the house beginning in 1866. The furnishings are worthy representatives of days gone by, uniformly rich and tasteful. Many are heirlooms; others have been collected by Mrs. Mitchell throughout the years to enhance the classic features of the old house and create an authentic picture of a fine ante bellum home.

The John Mark Verdier House

801 Bay Street
Owned by the Beaufort Historic Foundation, Inc.

John Mark Verdier was one of Beaufort's prominent merchant planters in the closing years of the eighteenth century. His father, Andrew, a French Huguenot refugee, had come to Beaufort by way of England, the West Indies, and the Swiss and Huguenot settlement at Purrysburg to teach in the Parish School from 1762 until 1764. His son, James Robert Verdier, was a physician and the builder of Marshlands. John Verdier was a shipbuilder with yards at Beaufort and Hilton Head Island and his vessels made regular runs to England with cargoes of rice, indigo, and cotton. Some of the shipments were produced on his own large Hilton Head Island plantations. Diverse merchandise making the the return trip to South Carolina included furnishing for Beaufort's fine town houses, and for the white clapboard house which he built for himself in the late 1790's.

The house has small double porticos with dentil molding trim on pediment and eaves. The traditional center hall divides it with a drawing room on the right, a dining room on the left, and two additional rooms to the rear. An elaborate be-columned archway in the hall frames a staircase leading to a landing with a Palladian window framed by reeded posts. From the landing a divided staircase continues to the upper hall. Across the front of the house a ballroom was built with an adjoining retiring room for the ladies. Dr. John A. Johnson has recorded in *Beaufort and the Sea Islands, Their History and Traditions* that the house was constructed by "Converse & Fish, northern mechanics, whose skill and industry secured them constant employment."

Viewing the quality of their craftsmanship a hundred and seventy-five years later, the thought may occur to visitors that these

"northern mechanics" might well have evoked the spirit of the master designer himself, Robert Adam, to guide them in their execution of refined and finished detail in mantels rich with allegorical figures, slender columns, ribbons, fruits, flowers, and sheaves of wheat and lavishly trimmed cornices and moldings.

When the Marquis de Lafayette arrived in Beaufort on his southern tour in 1825 the impressive Verdier house was one of the places he visited. The Lafayette party arrived by the inland passage from Charleston late in the evening of Friday the 18th of March. The citizens of Beaufort had been waiting since early that morning. When the *Henry Schultz* tied up at the dock at last a welcoming committee fired a thirteen-gun salute; bands began to play, and a procession was formed with the Beaufort Volunteer Artillery marching single file beside the carriages filled with dignitaries. Passing through a lighted triumphal arch they arrived at the Verdier house where William Elliott delivered a welcoming speech and Lafayette responded from the balcony overlooking the crowded street. The officials then moved on to Barnwell Castle for a grand ball. (Barnwell Castle, which burned in 1881, was on the site of the present Beaufort County Court House.) About three hours later the procession reformed and Lafayette was escorted back to his ship. The visit was short, but it had great impact and the Verdier house began to be called The Lafayette House. The Verdier family lived there until the Civil War when Union forces seized it for headquarters.

The old high-ceiling premises have witnessed varied business transactions for almost a hundred years. The drawing room with its inscrutable sphinxes on the mantel was a "tonsorial parlor." The ring of Beaufort's first telephone sounded in the ballroom above. The presses of *The Beaufort Gazette* were once located there and the basement has housed shops and a restaurant. By 1942 the building was in disrepair and it looked as though condemnation would be the end of its story. The Verdier heirs and William Levin generously relinquished their interests and it was purchased by public subscription to be preserved as a memorial to the sons of Beaufort who had given their lives for their country. Title was vested in The Beaufort Museum and a group of citizens administered the property. The outgrowth of these actions was the formation of Historic Beaufort Foundation, Inc., which acquired title to the house in 1968. As the John Mark Verdier House approaches the close of its second century its future looks bright. It is being restored, and the Foundation plans "the eventual total restoration and furnishing of this beautiful building as a House Museum, to be a reminder to our people of their cultural heritage and an attraction to our visitors."

The Lewis Reeve Sams House
601 Bay Street
Home of Mr. Lawrence Sanders

Just before the Beaufort River shifts its course northwestward to round Beaufort's storied Point, its waters wash the shores of a semicircle of land at the end of Bay Street where Lewis Reeve Sams, cotton planter of Datha Island, built a splendid Greek Revival town house in 1852. Two of his sons inherited it after his death in 1856.

Wide double verandas, Ionic and Doric pillars, spindled balustrades and meticulously carved dentil molding make it a prime example of the classic style so popular in the Low Country between 1815 and 1860.

The days of opulence and prosperity, with Sea Island long staple cotton selling for as much as $2.00 a pound, ended abruptly when Beaufort was occupied by Federal troops in 1861. The Sams family joined the exodus as the curtain came down on the saga of the planters. During the Civil War the house was Hospital No. 14 and was also used as quarters for officers of the Union Army. When the war was over Mr. Sams' sons redeemed it in 1869 with money borrowed from George Waterhouse. They later sold it to Mr. Waterhouse, grandfather of its present owner, Lawrence Sanders.

Today visitors to the house walk about on old wide floor boards made from the heart of long leaf pine, and admire carved door and window moldings crowned with stylized oak leaf medallions and ceilings fourteen feet high.

Twin settees upholstered in luxurious cut velvet stand in the center entrance hall extending a dignified welcome to callers. The hall is separated from a back hall and stairway by a shuttered partition and doorway. On the right is a parlor filled with unusual furniture such as an oak cathedral chair with red velvet cushions and a French sofa trimmed with gold braid and embroidery. To the right of a black marble mantel stands a fine nineteenth century needlepoint fire screen. The flower motif of the exquisite needlework is repeated in carved roses on the wooden frame.

The Clover Club was organized in this room by Mary Elizabeth Waterhouse in 1891. The club has an important place in the intellectual life of Beaufort with weekly programs being presented by its members. Since its formation the Clover Club has maintained a strong interest in the Beaufort County Library.

In the second drawing room of identical size across the hall there are handsome examples of Victorian furniture, a Spanish drop-end chair of green velvet piped in galloon which has adjustable flaps for comfort and warmth, and French pieces distinguished by intricate inlays. Standing tall are a pair of pressed glass candlesticks, which according to a family tradition were presented to the Marquis de Lafayette by George Washington, a fitting relic of the past for an old Beaufort home in view of the stir which was created by Lafayette's visit to the city in 1825.

The John Joyner Smith House

Wilmington and Bay
Home of Mr. and Mrs. Angus Fordham

A beautiful Greek Revival house built about 1813 by John Joyner Smith for his bride, Sarah Barnwell, still stands at the corner of Wilmington and Bay. The perfection and delicacy of its workmanship has lasted well, although it has had many owners since that bleak November day in 1861 when its builder fled with his family before the invading Federal troops.

The white frame house faces the silver waters of Beaufort Bay. Eight tall white pillars reach up three stories from a ground floor basement to support the roof. Slender balustrades on the upper and lower piazzas provide vertical contrast. Dentil molding trims the overhang of the roof. On the lower piazza a great false door was installed to heighten the elegant appearance of the house without robbing the drawing rooms within of space. Crowned with a wide, graceful doorhead and flanked by pilasters, it is an exercise in the effective use of contrasting vertical and horizontal lines enlivened by curves.

The entrance to the house is on the Wilmington Street side up curving marble steps to a door framed by reeded posts and side lights.

Twin drawing rooms across the front of the house have French windows leading onto the veranda and identical black Italian marble mantels. Round plaster medallions in the center of the ceilings are composed of roses entwined with leaves. The cornices have four rows of plaster designs in varying widths - acorns and oak leaves as white and fancified as a bride's headdress and showing to great advantage against walls of pale mauve.

John Joyner Smith also owned old Fort Plantation five miles away on the present site of the Naval Hospital. When Elizabeth Botume, a teacher from the New England Freedmen's Aid Society went there in 1864 to take up

quarters in the abandoned house and start a school for freed slaves she found some words on one of the posts of the front gallery which may have been written by the plantation's absent owner. It stated, according to Miss Botume in her *First Days Amongst the Contrabands,* "that for more than fifty years he had moved from this place to his house in town and back again, making the change over eighty times, and he devoutly thanked God for all the blessings he had received."

She further observed, "It seemed indescribably pathetic to me, thus to walk into a stranger's house and take quiet possession.

There was nothing within to remind one of the original owner. It was only when I walked around and saw the carefully arranged grounds, with fine shrubs and vines and graveled walks bordered with flowers, that I realized what the place had been. In spite of years of neglect - for it was first left to the care of the Negroes and then taken by the Union troops and used for soldiers' barracks and hospitals - in spite of all this, there was much beauty left. As I walked around, I was more than overwhelmed by a realization of the cruel necessities of a civil war . . ."

John Joyner Smith's town house was occupied by General Isaac Ingalls Stevens, commander of the Federal forces occupying Beaufort, his family and his staff.

Scholarly General Stevens tried to preserve the property of the town's absent owners, forbade plundering, and protested the plan Treasury Agents had to sell the contents of the Beaufort Library. The books were sent to New York for sale, anyhow. Although the sale was later cancelled, the books were lost to Beaufort

forever, as they burned while in storage at the Smithsonian Institution in Washington.

The general had his picture taken on the wide veranda surrounded by members of his staff with the massive false door serving as a sunlit background. John Joyner Smith was not able to redeem his holdings. All of his property was sold for taxes. "Lot A in Block 115 in Beaufort, South Carolina," with its fine house, luxuriant garden, detached kitchen, and Negro quarters went to Stephen Millet for $3,800 in 1865.

Forty years and four owners later it became the property of the Reverend C. C. Brown of Sumter, South Carolina, who also owned the Edgar Fripp House on Laurens Street, now known as Tidalholm. He called his property at Wilmington and Bay "The Colonial" and wrote to Mr. W. H. McLeod of Seabrook in 1910 that he would sell either house to him for the same price. Mr. McLeod's daughter, Mrs. Angus Fordham who lives in The Colonial now, recalls that her mother had a hard time deciding between two such appealing dwellings, but finally chose the one overlooking the Bay and roadway so that she could sit on the porch and watch the carriages pass by.

The McLeod Family moved from Seabrook to Beafort in 1915. The house has continued in the hands of Mr. and Mrs. Fordham, charmingly furnished with old family furniture, meticulously cared for, with the deeds, correspondence and records of ownership preserved. Even the photograph of General Isaac Stevens can still be seen. Sarah Barnwell Smith would probably feel very much at home, except, of course, for the photograph of the General.

The Robert Means House

1207 Bay Street
Home of Mrs. J. C. Sammons

Cotton displaced indigo as a staple crop on the plantations around Beaufort in the early 1800's, and in this pleasant era, when peace and pros-

perity had returned to the Sea Islands after the disruptions of the Revolution, Robert Means, prominent merchant and planter, built an attractive and dignified house.

Today a double stairway leads to a wide veranda and a front entrance door framed by a graceful fanlight. To the right of a center hall the luxuriously furnished drawing room contains some of Beaufort's most notable woodwork. The Adam mantel has elaborate swags, draperies, trailing vinery, and Grecian urns. A frieze in a delicate and orderly diamond pattern adorns the upper walls of the room.

The dining room, which is on the left of the center hall, has a plain deal mantel painted white. Its simplicity presents no distraction to the enjoyment of a dramatic original Audubon print of an eagle's nest hanging above it, nor of a beflowered needlepoint fire screen below. Elegant adjuncts to gracious living are displayed in the dining room, among them a large turkey platter with an engraved silver dome displaying the Luther family crest emblazoned with lion heads, and a great brass-bound wine cooler with representations of the same beast on its handles.

A mahogany staircase with slender rails leads to a landing and a sitting room at the back of the house. This room has an exceptionally fine carved dentil ceiling molding and a Palladian window overlooking the garden. The stairway continues to an upper hall and two bedrooms. These rooms and the upper piazza have their own breathtaking view of the watery splendor of the Beaufort River.

Mrs. J. C. Sammons, daughter of the late Mr. and Mrs. Charles G. Luther, who lived there for more than twenty years, maintains the traditions of the old house and treasures its many relics of the past including the Luther family tree which traces her ancestors back to Martin Luther, and a Bible from the year 1533 translated into German by the Great Reformer himself.

Tabby Manse

The Thomas Fuller House
1211 Bay Street
Home of Mr. and Mrs. George Trask

Thomas Fuller, forebear of one of Beaufort's most distinguished families, arrived from Charleston in 1788. He married Elizabeth Middleton, step-daughter of General Stephen Bull. Soon thereafter - the exact date is not known - he built a house remniscent of a great English country manor of tabby, or *tapia real,* a building material borrowed from the Spaniards. Early sea islanders used the durable mixture of crushed oyster shells, lime and sand extensively instead of brick or stone for dwellings, fortifications, indigo vats, cisterns, and sea walls.

The tabby walls of Thomas Fuller's house, eighteen to twenty inches thick, are covered with plaster scored to resemble stone. The effects of time and the elements have created a coloration of beige tinged with pink to set off the green shutters and white trim of the house which stands tall above a high basement. From the upper and lower porticos the sweep of the Beaufort River girdled by a crescent of green may be seen.

The center entrance hall which bisects the house has twin drawing rooms on each side. A stair hall at the rear opens into a bedroom and a dining room. A single wide stairway leads to a landing illuminated by a Palladian window where it divides and continues as two separate flights to the upper hall. Throughout the house there is extensive use of wood trim in wainscotings, moldings and paneling. Adam mantels display mythical casts of characters with style and distinction. The cognoscenti regard the mantel in the dining room as particularly fine with its deeply gouged horizontal and vertical channelings framing a Grecian urn.

The walls of the twin drawing rooms are paneled in heart of pine. In the one on the right

the paint has been stripped away permitting the flowing grain of the wood to emerge in the spacious tall-windowed room. The drawing room on the left is painted white. The upper floor has three large bedrooms and a ballroom as well which are finished with the same refined details which characterize "Tabby Manse."

Thomas Fuller was a merchant and planter with large land holdings near Sheldon which had been inherited by his wife. The house in Beaufort was the year-round residence of the family. One of his sons was Richard Fuller, the noted Baptist minister. Another was Dr.

Thomas Fuller who owned 2,550 acres of land on St. Helena Island in 1860.

During the War Between the States the house was used as a hospital. For many years after it passed from the hands of the Fuller family it was a guest house and the home of Clara and Alma Greenwood.

In 1969 Mr. and Mrs. George Trask bought it and have set about painting, repairing, reclaiming its original pine flooring from an accumulation of brown paint, and selecting furnishings compatible with the august characteristics of the old home.

The Edward Barnwell House

1405 Bay Street
Home of Mr. and Mrs. G. G. Dowling

For more than a century and a half the Edward Barnwell House on The Bay has kept silent watch over the tidal currents of the Beaufort River flowing past its door. On a May day in 1819 it was a witness when a gala ten-oared canoe provided by the Town Council of Beaufort went by, oars flashing, bearing the "Chief Magistrate of the Union," tall, stooped James Monroe, fifth President of the nation, pausing in the Low Country on a tour of the South. And in 1825 its imposing presence lent distinction to the river bluff when the Marquis de Lafayette came for a visit which is still remembered. In those times and later it provided a view through its great windows of red-jacketed negro slaves propelling heavy row boats with planter fishermen going out for devil fish or drum, brightening the surface of the water and filling the air with melancholy song:

> *"Oh, your soul! Oh, my soul! I'm*
> *goin' to de churchyard to lay dis*
> *body down;*
> *Oh, my soul! Oh, your soul! We're*
> *goin' to de churchyard to lay dis*
> *body down."*

The house was built around 1815 by Edward Barnwell, great-grandson of legendary Tuscorora Jack Barnwell, the Indian fighter and statesman.

Edward Barnwell's toast on the occasion of Beaufort's celebration of the Fourth of July in 1819 has been recorded: "The memory of General Alexander Hamilton, truly the favorite of both Minervas." Barnwell had seventeen children and three wives. His son had seventeen children and one wife. A visitor's comment about the many, many Barnwells buried in St. Helena's churchyard prompted the sexton, who was acting as guide, to reply,

"Yes ma'am, dem sho' was a powerful nation."

The sentinel on the bluff has mellowed with the years and been the object of some alterations. Its many-pillared double verandas have been replaced by a single portico and four rounded columns which support the pedimented roof. There have been changes in the interior such as the removal of one of the staircases and some of the mantels and paneling. However, the authentic flavor of a fine house of the old era is preserved in the many cherished Adam features which remain. Radiant sunlight streams through an original Palladian window on the stair landing. The drawing room with pale blue walls and white wainscoting has its Adam mantel with a trio of carved eagles and beadwork trim.

Members of the Barnwell family probably lived in the house until the Civil War. During the war it was a Signal Station and United States Military Telegraph Office. After the War it was sold for taxes. In the early 1900's it was owned by Maude O'Dell of Beaufort who had a great success on Broadway as an actress in *Tobacco Road*. Before being purchased by Mr. and Mrs. Dowling it was the home of Mr. and Mrs. Peter B. Cohen and earlier the home of Mr. and Mrs. J. E. McTeer.

Secession House

The Edmund Rhett House
1113 Craven Street
Home of Mr. and Mrs. Claude McLeod

Secession House, since 1953 the home of Mr. and Mrs. Claude McLeod, was once the setting for firebrand political activities when it belonged to Edmund Rhett, brother of United States Senator Robert Barnwell Rhett, who was called the "father of Secession." An inscription on the basement wall reads, "In this house the first meeting in favor of secession was held in 1851." British journalist William Howard wrote of Edmund Rhett in April 1861: "He declared that there were few persons in South Carolina who would not sooner ask Great Britain to take back the State than to submit to the triumph of the Yankees."

The two lots on which the house stands were granted to Robert Williams around 1743. It is believed that a two-story tabby dwelling was built on the site before the Revolution and that Milton Maxcy, who came to South Carolina from Massachusetts around 1800 to open a school for boys, removed the tabby second floor and added two stories of wood.

Before the middle of the nineteenth century Edmund Rhett rebuilt the two upper floors completely and fashioned the house's present aspect of modified Greek revival architecture, preserving the old basement with its solid walls of tabby.

Curved white marble steps with wrought iron balustrades lead to a lower veranda with Ionic columns and dentil moldings, above which is an upper veranda with columns of the Corinthian order. A drawing of the house made during the Civil War shows a parapet around the roof, but it is gone now.

East and west of the center hall are twin drawing rooms with intricate cornice work and plaster medallions which bring to mind old-fashioned lace paper valentines. The rooms have variegated marble mantels of Italian

Verde. The Beaufort County Delegation met in the east room in 1851 to support South Carolina's secession from the Union.

Mrs. McLeod has furnished her home with antiques and family pieces such as an 1841 mahogany secretary with an inlaid rope design and an old hickory chair circa 1714 which was carved from the tongue of a wagon. She has adorned its walls with marine pictures by Mr. McLeod's grandfather and oil paintings of flowers by Mr. McLeod's mother.

Union soldiers who occupied the house in December 1861 have left behind notations of names, home towns, regiments, and sentiments such as "Union Forever" crowned by the drawing of an eagle on the walls of the old tabby basement. Also uncovered when accumulated

paint was removed from the walls is a notice reading "Paymaster Department." The house was once the office of the U. S. Direct Tax Commission for South Carolina.

Back of the house stands an old kitchen building with an immense chimney which bears on its worn bricks the beveling of knives sharpened there by the many cooks who used it as a handy whetstone. (Before her death in 1968, Beaufort novelist Ann Head who lived at Battery Creek, used the old kitchen as a writing retreat.)

The William Fickling House
Rectory of St. Helena's Episcopal Church
1109 Craven Street
Home of the Reverend John W. and Mrs. Hardy

"Small, old, cold, and uncomfortable, but we had some merry times in it," said W. G. Reed - on duty in Beaufort during the Civil War occupation - of the neat, compact, white frame house built in the early 1800's by William Fickling, headmaster of a school for boys. If Critic Reed could return from his grave, he would find this interesting home older but today truly pleasant and comfortable. Since 1894 it has been the Rectory of St. Helena's Episcopal Church and as an inviting and livable home tenanted for the past seventeen years by the Reverend John W. and Mrs. Hardy. Mrs. Hardy is no stranger to old houses. Her ancestral home in Edenton, North Carolina, dates back to 1838.

Resting on a latticed basement, the house is approached by brick steps leading to a wide porch with slender, tapered columns stretching up to a second floor veranda. Earlier steps, as seen in an 1865 photograph taken by Mr. Reed, and deposited by him at the Beaufort County Library, were at right angles to the front door.

Originally one room deep, the house was enlarged after the Civil War by an addition at the rear. Wainscoting and dentil molding at the

top of the walls of the drawing room at the east date back to the original construction. A handsome black marble mantel in this room is a later addition. Among the interesting furnishings are carpets from Central Asia. Of Particular interest to the conoisseur is a rare Baluchi rug with a background of blue instead of the purple and red tones usually found in the work of its nomadic weavers. In addition there is a Yomud rug with rich rose coloring and a Turcoman of Pinde' design. A cane bottomed sewing chair with a spindled back invites a restful pause to enjoy Chopin and Mendelsson Melodies trickling from an old music box which the Reverend Mr. Hardy found in England when he was stationed there as a chaplain during World War II.

Mr. Hardy, whose sense of history as Rector is in complete harmony with the traditions of a church such as St. Helena's, has an important collection of old books. Among them is a copy of *Prayers of the Church and Reflections on the Liturgy* published in Philadelphia in 1839 and written by his distinguished predecessor, the Reverend Joseph R. Walker, D. D., who came to Beaufort as a young priest in 1823 and remained for fifty-five years, and a *Book of Common Prayer* printed in London in 1804.

Tabernackle Baptist Church
Craven Street Between Charles and West

This white and venerable tall steepled wooden building has been in service since 1811. The congregation of the Baptist Church of Beaufort maintained it as a lecture room early in the nineteenth century and worshipped there temporarily while the present church building was under construction from 1842 to 1844.

It was organized as a separate church by the Reverend Solomon Peck, of Boston, Massachusetts, in 1863 for negro members who withdrew from The Baptist Church of Beaufort during the Civil War. Following damage by a storm in 1890 portions were rebuilt and repaired keeping to the original style. An early gravestone in the church yard is dated 1815. Robert Smalls, the slave who became a congressman, is buried here near a large mulberry tree with his first wife, Hannah, on his right and his second wife, Annie, on his left.

The Roman Catholic Church of St. Peter the Apostle
Duke and Carteret Streets

Michael O'Connor arrived in the Carolina Low Country in 1822. Beneath skies as blue as those of his native Ireland he prospered as a builder and mechanic in Beaufort, marrying Mary Lake, who was converted to join him in the practice of the Roman Catholic faith. From time to time a priest would make the long two-to-three-day journey from Charleston to say masses in the O'Connor home and perform baptisms as needed.

In 1846 O'Connor built the Church of St. Peter the Apostle, using his own resources, and bequeathed it to the diocese. Although the sanctuary has been greatly enlarged and a porch and pillars have been removed from the front of the building to be replaced by a small

porch with brick steps and a wrought iron railing, the church remains essentially as Michael O'Connor created it - a starkly simple white frame Colonial type building, an eloquent expression of a devout immigrant's faith and thanksgiving. In 1857 Franklin Talbird, master mason of Beaufort and builder of the Edward Means House at 604 Pinckney Street, contributed the design, labor, and materials for the brick wall which encloses the church and its grounds.

The front of the building has a gable surmounted by a cross. A smaller cross rises from a broken pediment set above the entrance door. There are five rectangular stained glass windows on each side of the building and two on the front, all of which were installed in 1864. The church has a center aisle with a confessional on the right and choir stalls on the left. The statues and sanctuary lamp date from 1921, the altar and its Gothic window from 1928.

Michael O'Connor, his wife and several of their children are buried in the cemetery behind the church he built.

O God
We Acknowledge
Thee to be
The Lord

St. Helena's Episcopal Church

Church Street Between King and North

A small group of colonists in the village of Beaufort founded this hallowed old church in 1712 in a time of great troubles. However, members of the devout little band who regarded as an assurance of Divine protection the fact that the Great Carolina Hurricane of 1713 missed Beaufort and destroyed Charleston instead, were doomed to a tragic surprise. For the troubles were of human origin and more sinister than the storms that boiled up from the Caribbean. They were caused by the Yamassee Indians, and two years later, as the colonists, meeting for religious services in private homes, made plans for building a church, the Yamassees destroyed the town, killing many settlers and forcing the rest to disperse.

The striving for a church persisted and in 1724 the wardens and vestrymen of the Parish of St. Helena of Granville (now Beaufort) County sent to the Lord Bishop of London a "humble petition" for a "sober and learned person to be our minister. We being a frontier parish and most of our people inclineable to the Church, but for want of injoying the blessing of the gospel and public worship as by law established, they are daily tempted and led away." They also informed the Bishop that a handsome brick church was nearly completed. The Lord Bishop granted the request, and in due time the Reverend Mr. Lewis Jones, consigned from Wales, arrived on the scene.

The first structure was enlarged and rebuilt in 1817 and again in 1842. Each time the designers and builders proceeded with respect for beauty, simplicity and noble proportions and the spirit of the early Colonial church architecture has been well preserved.

Built of brick covered with cement stucco, it has many small-paned windows, each one

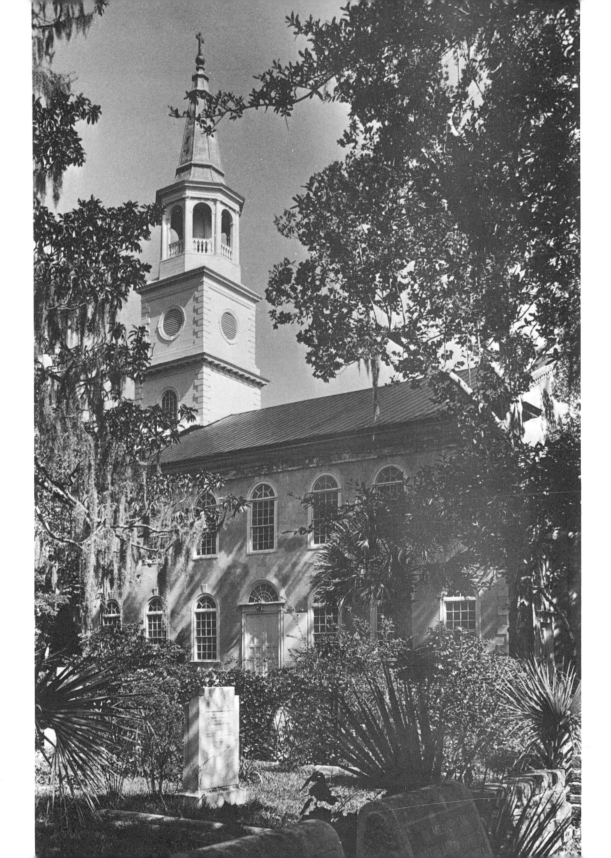

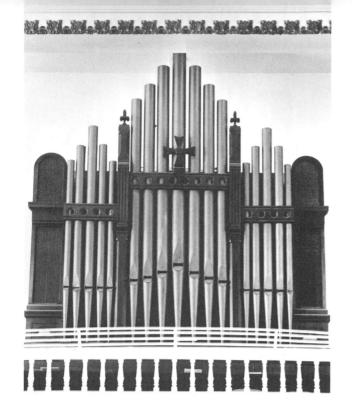

Michael's and St. Philip's churches of that many-spired city.

The white painted interior has elaborate cornices trimmed in gold, simple white columns and graceful balconies. It is the setting for a rich heritage of memories of stirring events.

Lovingly cared for by the Altar Guild of the Church are a silver chalice with the emblem of the Crown of Thorns, a paten and a small alms basin which Captain John Bull gave in memory of his wife who disappeared at the sad Eastertime of 1715 when the Yamassees raided the city.

The floor of the church covers the grave of John (Tuscarora Jack) Barnwell, fiery Irishman turned Indian fighter, who arrived in South Carolina in 1701, commanded a successful expedition to subdue the Tuscarora Indians in North Carolina in 1711, and has been dead and buried since 1724.

John and Charles Wesley visited Beaufort in 1736. In 1737 John was the guest of the rector of St. Helena's, who, he reported, gave him "a lively idea of the old English hospitality."

In 1832 the impact of a Revival held in Beaufort was felt at home and in the four corners of the world as well. The Reverend Joseph R. Walker, who was rector at the time, invited the Reverend Daniel Baker, a Presbyterian evangelist to come and preach in Beaufort. Services were held alternately at St. Helena's and at the Baptist Church of Beaufort. A great surge of religious feeling influenced large numbers to enter the ministry, many as missionaries.

During the Civil War the church was used as a hospital with its flat tombstones serving as operating tables.

Illustrious dead resting in the church yard include soldiers, sailors, statesmen, writers, and ministers. They all lie, with many unidentified tenants, shaded by dogwood, wisteria, palms, and a cedar tree brought from Lebanon in 1825 by the Reverend Dr. Walker.

crowned with a fanlight. The steeple was removed just before the Civil War when it was discovered to be structurally unsound. A new steeple was added in 1941, designed by Albert Simons of Charleston in the style of St.

BEAUFORT BAPTIST CHURCH
ORGANIZED A. D. 1800.
THIS BUILDING ERECTED IN 1844
DURING THE PASTORATE OF
RICHARD FULLER, D. D.
PASTOR OF THIS CHURCH 1833-1847
*ABOVE ALL BE FAITHFUL TO CHRIST
AND HIS TRUTH*

The Baptist Church of Beaufort
600 Charles Street

One wintry day in January 1804 the congregation of The Baptist Church of Euhaw, across Broad River eight miles from Beaufort, gathered in solemn assembly to sign an Act of Incorporation, involving the transformation of its mission in Beaufort with property on the islands of Port Royal, west of Beaufort, and St. Helena, into a new church to be established in Beaufort.

The fledgling church, composed of eighteen white members and numerous Negro slaves who formerly attended the mission, rapidly became a power to be reckoned with in the moral life of the community - excommunicating, suspending, censuring, disciplining, or rebuking its occasionally errant members, white and black. On February 12, 1842 it "resolved that this church regards attendance at Theaters or Circuses and similar scenes as grossly inconsistent with the character and deportment becoming its members and will always consider the same as a sin calling for prompt discipline."

Early church records chronicle an active concern for the religious and social life of the Negro slaves with funds being distributed for

restored to use, as was the communion table, which was retrieved from the Freedman's Bureau in Charleston. A few of the pews were found in an Episcopal lecture room in Beaufort and brought back.

The present church building was completed in 1844 during the ministry of Richard Fuller, who had renounced the profession of law for the ministry under the impact of the powerful preaching of Presbyterian Evangelist Daniel Baker during the Beaufort Revival of 1832.

In 1842 Pastor Fuller bemoaned that "a calamity of an uncommon kind has befallen us." The church was sagging in the middle from the stress of defective walls and roof. He set about to raise money for a new church with such zeal and persistence that he earned for himself a new title - "The Pince of Beggars."

The architecture of the Baptist Church of Beaufort has been attributed to nationally acclaimed Robert Mills of Charleston, architect of the Treasury Building in Washington and the Washington Monument. If the plans were not drawn by Robert Mills, a close friend of Dr. Fuller, the building is very much in the Mills tradition and has many features which are characteristic of his genius. It is austere, "sternly beautiful" in the Greek Revival style. The exterior columns and the double columns which support the balconies within are simplified Doric which Mills preferred. The severe Greek key design over the door is one of the simple symbols he used effectively. Plasterwork on the gently curving ceiling depicts acanthus leaves in high relief.

The work of a masterful hand and mind is evident in the building's harmonious lines and proportions. A solid pediment rises above tall white columns at the entrance. The steeple has its own smaller pediments, and ends in a slender spire. Throughout the edifice roundheaded windows and rounded inserts add graceful fluid lines. On sunny days the hallowed building gleams like alabaster.

their aid and relief. They were baptized, received into membership, and they worshiped along with their white masters. Separate missions under the charge of lay preachers were set up for their use as the congregation grew.

All of the 166 whites and some of the 3,557 Negroes listed on the church rolls in 1861 scattered when Beaufort was occupied by Union forces. Groans of sick and wounded displaced the "joyful noise" of worship and singing when it was converted into a military hospital. A second floor was added extending from the side balconies. At the war's end it had been stripped of its pulpit, communion table, and pews, and was in a very dilapidated state. However, one of the colored deacons, Jacob Whittier, had safeguarded the hymn books and communion service and they were

The Frederick Grimke Fraser House

901 Prince Street
Home of Mrs. Maurice Matteson

This towering old house with green shutters and a red roof dates back to the early 1800's and was built by Frederick Grimke Fraser, relative of the well-known Charleston painter, Charles Fraser, and a descendent of John Fraser, stout Scotsman, who ventured into the New World around 1700 to settle at Pocotaligo near the Coosawhatchee River where the Yamassee Indians were wont to assemble in tribal council. It has been asserted by Dr. J. Chapman Milling that this immigrant ancestor flogged his Indian slaves, sold free Indians to the Spaniards at St. Augustine, and that the Indians bore him no love. It has also been recorded that his wife, Judith Warner, a Rhode Islander, was of a gentler disposition. Perhaps that is why a member of the Yamassee tribe named Sanute gave warning of the bloody uprising of 1715, enabling the family to escape.

Sturdily constructed of brick covered with white stucco and rising two floors above a high basement, the Fraser house has upper and lower verandas across the front, each with six fluted columns and enclosed by low wooden bannisters. The doorway leading from the upstairs hall to the veranda is Palladian. Throughout the house the woodwork is in the simple style characteristic of its period with graceful mantels and cornices, wainscoting formed of boards twenty inches wide, and panelled doors.

Frederick Fraser's heirs lost the Beaufort house during the upheaval of the Civil War. After the war they were able to recover it only briefly from 1875 until 1883 when it was sold by a court order. Joshua Whitman bought it and deeded it to his daughter, Mrs. Harold A. Bristol in 1907. Mr. Bristol was mayor of Beaufort in the early years of this century. It remained the home of the Bristols until 1953

when the late Dr. Maurice Matteson and Mrs. Matteson saw it and chose it as a retirement home and a depository for their treasured collections of antique furniture, china, glass, books, old music (including first editions of the works of Stephen Foster), and musical instruments.

The house is two rooms deep on the first floor, one on the second floor. To the right of a center hall flooded with light from a large window on the stair landing and the Palladian door there is a spacious drawing room. Mirrors with gold leaf frames, a crystal chandelier and oil paintings set the scene for rich furnishings which include carved tables, a Victorian sofa covered in red velvet, a grand piano, and a melodion. The melodion was made in Worcester, Massachusetts, in the early nineteenth century. An informal sitting room and library back of the drawing room has its own grand piano. Across the hall there is a dining room of

ample proportions and noble woodwork, and a guest bedroom.

To Dr. and Mrs. Matteson, as musicians and lifelong teachers of music, the small rectangular blocks incorporated into the designs of the moldings of the ceilings and outside trim of the eaves which are described as dentil suggested not teeth, according to Mrs. Matteson, but piano keys. Mrs. Matteson continues the loving care and preservation of the old house and garden, with its abundant tropical plantings of loquat, hawthorne, palmettos, and myrtle, which she and her husband began together. She opens her home to visitors during the St. Helena's Episcopal Church spring tours and displays along with the important collection of old music two books of folklore music which bear the name of Dr. Matteson, *Beech Mountain Ballads* and *American Folk Songs for Young Children*.

The Henry McKee House

511 Prince Street
Home of Captain and Mrs. Charles N. Barnum

In a quiet setting behind a lacework wall of ivy-draped bricks this old house, built for Henry McKee, cotton planter around 1823 by his father, John, has survived the death of an opulent era, witnessed the epoch of a destructive civil war, and weathered the buffetings of time and the elements with its impressive dignity unimpaired.

Acquired in 1963 by Captain and Mrs. Charles Barnum, the house today is an attractive two-storied, white frame, green shuttered dwelling resting on tall tabby foundations. The old boards of the verandas have been scraped of paint and gleam like the deck of a ship through clear varnish.

Inside the house the original woodwork is intact as are the amber toned boards of old pine floors. Cherished heirlooms of the families of both Captain and Mrs. Barnum as well as their own distinctive later acquisitions are displayed.

Over the fireplace in the drawing room hangs a portrait of Mrs. Barnum painted by John Nielson. Reeded supports of the Adam mantel and a fan design incorporated into the carving are carried almost to the top of the twelve-and-one-half-foot ceiling forming a unique frame for the portrait.

Notable in the drawing room is a mahogany chair, a German interpretation of the French Empire style of the mid-nineteenth century, with carved allegorical figures. The adornments of brass *applique* show fine detail work of leaves, flowers, and classic faces. Beside the fireplace is a rosewood veneer console table of the same period with a low mirror for the ladies of the day who wished to check the hang of their crinolines.

The size of the room allows the graceful arrangement of two sofas and a grand piano.

One of the sofas is flanked by a pair of tables with hinged glass tops and a collection of articles of vertu including family miniatures, pre-Columbian clay figures, and carved jade. There is a cup and saucer of Lowestoft from which George Washington drank tea when he paused to refresh himself at the home of one of the Captain's ancestors at Hunt's Point on Long Island, New York. Mr. Hunt had the foresight to put it away carefully, forbidding its use to other and less distinguished sippers and it has come down through the years as a family treasure.

The dining room is to the right of a wide center hall. Over an Adam mantel in this room hangs an old print of the *Sovereign of the Seas* which was afloat in 1637. It now keeps company with a maple New England dundee chest from the same century.

Upstairs two bedrooms divided by a hall blend antiques and reproductions. A carved wooden spaniel rising from the pedestal of a marble topped mid-Victorian table guards a wickerwork trunk covered with leather which once transported the hoop skirts of an ancestress on her honeymoon journey.

A New England desk of pine has scrimshaw type carving evoking the ghost of some old beached sea dog absorbed in his intricate work. A pair of seventeenth-century pine chairs with high backs and wings to shield against the icy winds of New England add a note of appealing simplicity.

Both Captain and Mrs. Barnum are gifted painters and they have exhibited not only their own work, but those of their many artist friends throughout the house.

In the garden behind the house the tabby foundations of an old cabin may be seen. A slave boy named Robert Smalls was born here in the days when Henry McKee and his family enjoyed the quiet of peaceful afternoons on the breeze swept veranda.

Twelve years later the boy was hired out in Charleston by his master as a lamplighter. Over a period of years he progressed to better jobs and eventually became the pilot of the *Planter,* a shallow draft coastal vessel chartered by the Confederacy to move men, arms, and supplies. The Civil War was scarcely a year old when Robert Smalls made a plan to gain freedom for himself and his family - a plan as secret and shadowy as the inner reaches of the coastal waterway he knew so well.

On a misty morning in May with his wife and two children hidden aboard, he and some of the crewmen slipped out of Charleston Harbor under the guns of the Confederate forts, reached the blockading squadron of the Union Fleet, and turned over the *Planter,* its own armaments, four extra cannon lashed to the deck, and vital information about nearby Confederate fortifications. Three years later Robert Smalls was master of the ship on which he had served as a slave.

In 1865 he bought for $700 the house at 511 Prince Street, which had been confiscated by the Federal Government from Richard DeTreville who had acquired the house from the McKees before the war began. He lived there until his death in 1915. Members of his family owned it until 1950.

Robert Smalls had suffered no ill treatment from the McKees. It had been the condition of slavery which had rankled him. During the years of "Reconstruction" he was a congressman from South Carolina and one of the first measures he introduced in 1875 was a "bill for the relief of Henry McKee and his heirs."

1 Washington Street

*Home of Miss Abby W. Christensen and
Mrs. Neils Christensen, Jr.*

Shielded by semitropical foliage beside the Beaufort River, this house, rising two stories from an arched basement, exhibits many of the unique and beautiful attributes of a Sea Island home. Wide verandas with slender posts and spindled balustrades stretch away on three sides.

Lena Wood Lengnick in *Beaufort Memoirs* states that it was built as a parsonage for Henry Ledbetter, a Methodist minister in 1805 or 1806, but the first verified ownership is that of William Baynard who sold it to Thomas Talbird in 1838. From that time it had several owners until Captain Neils Christensen purchased it in 1881 from George Holmes, a busy Yankee trader in Beaufort real estate after the Civil War. It has been known as the Christensen House ever since.

Captain Christensen was a handsome young Dane who arrived in the United States at the beginning of the Civil War and served in the Union Army for four years. Part of his military service was spent in Beaufort. When the war was over he returned as superintendent of the National Cemetery. A few years later he married Abbie Holmes, daughter of an official of the Freedman's Bureau. Captain Christensen beautified the National Cemetery with extensive plantings of native trees and created a remarkable display of exotic trees and shrubs on the large grounds surrounding his home. He was active in the formation of a Methodist Church in Beaufort in 1884.

The high ceilinged rooms of the house, distinguished by paneled doors and decorative moldings, open off of a center hall. Many of the furnishings are New England antiques from the family of Mrs. Neils Christensen, Sr. Others, such as paintings in high-wrought gold-leaf frames and a black marble oval table with a luminous inlay of morning glories, lilies, and forget-me-nots, were gathered by members of the family on European journeys.

Miss Abby W. Christensen, Captain Christensen's daughter lives in the old house at the present time.

701 Green Street

Home of Mr. and Mrs. Ellis DeTreville

Another example of an old house which has outlived the recording of the name of the man who built it is at the corner of Carteret and Green Streets. (It has been speculated that it was built by a member of the Baker family of planters of St. Helena Island.) A clue to its age may be found in the name of its first known occupant, the Reverend James Graham, a Scotsman who was pastor of the Baptist Church of Beaufort between 1819 and 1831. The frame house is raised on foundations of brick and tabby and has double verandas set off by plain posts and banisters.

During the Civil War and its aftermath it was filled with a stir and bustle created by teachers and missionaries from the North as they went about their business of working for the welfare of the freed slaves, singing hymns and *John Brown's Body* and quoting John Greenleaf Whittier:

*"We go to rear a wall of men
On Freedom's southern line
And plant beside the cotton tree
The rugged Northern pine!"*

Francis George Shaw, an official of the New York National Freedman's Aid Society, bought it in 1864. A wrought iron gate with the words, "American Missionary Association," had been left as a reminder of its designation as Mission House. Mrs. Rachel Crane Mather of Boston was another of its occupants. In 1868 she established a school for Negro girls sponsored by the American Baptist Home mission society which was the forerunner of The Mather School of Beaufort.

Since 1925 it has been the home of Mr. and Mrs. Ellis DeTreville. Mr. DeTreville is a descendant of John Labouladrie DeTreville whose coming to South Carolina as a very young boy in 1755 recalls the little known story of more than a thousand Acadians exiled

from their homes in Nova Scotia and forcibly transported to South Carolina. Many left and many died, but John Labouladrie DeTreville remained to fight for his adopted state in the Revolution as a volunteer, rising to the rank of Captain in the Fourth Artillery Regiment of South Carolina Line, Continental Establishment.

The John Hazel House

Northeast corner of New and North Streets
Home of Mr. and Mrs. William Bowen

This beautiful three-story home, built in 1852 by John (or possibly Tom) Hazel for his bride is also known as the Hazel-Foster house, in recognition of another bride. During the War Between The States it was used as a hospital. Etta Foster moved into the house in 1904 as the wife of Captain John Sydney Foster. The property was put in her name as a wedding present from the Captain. After the latter's death more than 30 years ago, Mrs. Foster locked up their home and moved across the street into the house of her niece. It remained closed until 1969 when it was bought and restored by Mr. and Mrs. William Bowen.

The house has changed little through the years. It is one of the few buildings in Beaufort with an original parapet matching the railings on each porch. The rooms are extended onto the porch by dutch doors. There are three dormer windows across the front and overhead stand two huge chimneys with the three-piece or "pot" tops.

The West room off the central hallway displays a handsome white marble mantelpiece, and the East room has an equally attractive mantelpiece of black marble. The stairs retain their original mahogany rails and banisters.

The Walker/Knott House

401 King Street
(The "Little Taj")

Built in accord with the style of many of the larger homes of the Point, this old house is smaller than most. Situated opposite the "Pond" it offers a charming vista through the trees to the river in the distance. The spell of the view of the house from Federal Street across the lagoon in bright moonlight led some of the Point dwellers to dub it the "Little Taj" with all respect to the marble Taj Mahal of India.

The designation of the Walker/Knott house stems from its ownership by Emily Walker who sold it to Margaret Knott in 1933. As with the larger homes it was built to gain full benefit of the southern winds, and has porches at the front both downstairs and on the second floor. To utilize the breezes throughout, small wings were constructed from each side of the house at the rear. The interior has a central stairway leading from the small entrance hall. There are fireplaces in all the rooms with the old brick still in place. The front walk is constructed of various types of rock and brick including two round porous stones resembling millstones. Courthouse records indicate that the house was built in 1856, but it is possibly older since there are local unconfirmed stories that it may have been standing in 1823, the home of Miss Jane Bonds who married Henry Mckee, for whom the house at 511 Prince Street was built.

The house was purchased in 1969 by Elizabeth Cole who resides with her husband in another restored house at 601 Prince Street.

Other Old Buildings of Interest

University of South Carolina

Beaufort Regional Campus
800 Carteret Street

Established as a branch of the University of South Carolina in 1959, this building, constructed in 1852, was one of the several homes of Beaufort College, incorporated in 1795. The cornerstone of the first building of the college on another location was laid November 4, 1802. From 1904 until World War II it was an elementary school.

The Beaufort Arsenal

Craven Street between Carteret and Scott

Behind a high brick wall and a sentinel row of palmettos, stands the old Beaufort Arsenal, cloaked in an aura of tradition. Constructed in 1798 on what is believed to be the site of an early powder magazine, it was rebuilt in 1852 after fire had severely damaged the upper story. Part of the lower structure with its heavy arches and cavernous rooms is original. For many years it served as the home of the Beaufort Volunteer Artillery, descendent of a 1776 volunteer militia company. During the Battle of Port Royal, November 7, 1861, the Beaufort Volunteer Artillery was stationed at Fort Beauregard under the command of Captain Stephen Elliott.

The Arsenal houses the Beaufort Museum. Among its many interesting relics of the past are a Huguenot sword dated 1562 which was unearthed on Parris Island and an ale pitcher once owned by Thomas Heyward, Jr., a signer of the Declaration of Independence.

The George Parsons Elliott House

1001 Bay Street
Owned by the Bank of Beaufort
(Known as the Bank of Beaufort - Hall House)

In restoring this home and making it accessible to visitors the Bank of Beaufort has performed a valuable public service. Those who wish to study the lines of an ante bellum stairway and ponder the decor of bygone days can do so at seasons other than spring when the Church-women of St. Helena's Episcopal Church conduct their tour of old Beaufort homes and nearby plantations.

In harmony with the concept of adaptive use of historic properties the bank is using the lower floor for offices and has restored the central floor as a house museum. It is available for concerts, art exhibits, and meetings.

The large house, with old-style verandas and tall white columns, was built by George Parsons Elliott around 1848. For many years it was suggested that it had been built elsewhere and moved to its present site. Recently a qualified expert made a careful inspection of its construction and stated that in his opinion it had not been moved but was built where it now stands overlooking the bay.

Confiscated from its owner, Dr. W. J. Jenkins, at the time of the Civil War, it was bought for taxes by George Holmes after an interval during the War when it was Federal Hospital No. 15. Dr. Jenkins could not reclaim his home, but he did manage to reclaim his waterfront view. He took the lumber from a barn which he owned and used it to build a frame house between his former home and the water. Old residents of Beaufort called it the "spite house" and recall that it was still standing in the early 1900's.

Many of the period furnishings such as the Sheraton dining table and Chippendale chairs in the dining room and the laquer and gold chairs and settees in the music room have been purchased by the bank. Others have been loaned by John Bennett of Mount Pleasant, South Carolina, grandson of John Bennett, author, poet, and illustrator who wrote *Master Skylark* and *Peyre Gaillard.* Many of the items loaned by Mr. Bennett have authenticated historical associations. An American Empire mahogany sideboard with carved pine cones and plumes on its front posts and brass lion head drawer pulls and a sofa, circa 1820 (both attributed to Duncan Phyfe), came from Lang Syne near Charleston, the plantation home of Joseph Dulles, an ancestor of John Foster Dulles. The Sheffield candelabra on the dining room table once shed their light at Lang Syne, which was built by Langdon Cheves, Carolina statesman and orator of the 19th century. The house was destroyed during Sherman's rampage through the Low Country in 1865 but the candlesticks were hidden in a cistern and later recovered.

The center hall has an archway crowned with a delicate mullioned fanlight which is repeated over the entrance door. A gold trimmed chandelier hanging from a rococco plaster cartouche and a frieze of golden grapes set off by white walls and ceilings serve as a fitting sample of the elegance which characterizes the entire restoration.

Among the antique furnishings there are a grandfather clock from the year 1780 with wooden works, a triplex Adam mirror framed in gold leaf with a Wedgewood green and white motif; and a butler's desk of mahogany with notable brass fittings. These pieces are in the living room. The dining room contains an original Chippendale cellarette with brass handles and a snakewood inlay with many of its original Waterford bottles. Ormulu girandoles with cut rock crystal hanging prisms on the mantel shelf in the music room repeat the gold of the trim of the room's late Victorian furniture and in this room a square piano and a harp have been placed for concerts.

The home has a warm, lived-in look with many of the homely necessities from days long past, churns and spinning wheels, and guns and powder horns. There are fine china and silver, Catesby and Gould bird prints, antique embroidered silk panels and old leather editions of Charles Dickens' works.

The bank purchased the house in 1967 from Mr. and Mrs. L. A. Hall. Although it has restored the old home, it has not restored to it the name of its builder, George Parsons Elliott. It is called the Bank of Beaufort-Hall house. (Open from eleven to three Tuesdays, Wednesdays, Thursdays, Fridays and Saturdays and from two to five Sundays. Admission $1.00).

The William Elliott House

(The Anchorage)
1103 Bay Street

Although the date of its construction cannot be precisely established, this house - a very old one - was built either just before or just after the Revolution by William Elliott. Wade Hampton, ex-Confederate General and controversial political figure during Reconstruction, spoke from the porch during his successful campaign for the governorship of South Carolina in 1876.

Rear Admiral L. A. Beardsley, who owned it is 1890, named it "The Anchorage" as it was his retirement home. He made considerable alterations such as removing the original woodwork, adding brick fireplaces, and stuccoing the exterior. It was a guest house for many years and was sold in June of 1969 to Joe and Randall Horne for a restaurant.

The William Henry Trescott House

1011 Bay Street
Owned by Dr. and Mrs. W. A. Black

Built on Barnwell Island shortly before the Civil War by William Henry Trescott, this house was moved to its present location in 1876 by Colonel William Elliott. William Henry Trescott served as an *attache'* at the American Legation in London and was Undersecretary of State during the administration of President Buchanan. He was the author of *The History of American Diplomacy*. Most of the construction of the house was done by his slaves with finished paneling and window trim ordered from Charleston. It has been converted into offices.

The Edgar Fripp House

Tidalholm
1 Laurens Street

Bounded on three sides by water, Tidalholm - so called for the past thirty years - was built by Edgar Fripp, cotton planter of St. Helena's Island, in the late 1850's. As a unique and exclusive guest house it has been a mecca for distinguished writers, artists, and educators. The cornices and ceiling arabesques are dramatically beautiful.

The story is told that when the house was for sale for taxes after the Civil War a Frenchman who was passing through Beaufort bought it, gave it to the Fripp family, and bowed out without leaving an address. In September of 1969 the house was purchased by Mrs. Alida Harper Fowlkes of Savannah, Georgia who has an antique shop there and plans to refurbish Tidalhom and furnish it with period pieces.

Outlying Churches, Homes and Plantations

across the top of the building. Semicircular patterns of brick crown the doorways and windows. The only contrasting trim is the white of the doors and window frames.

During the Civil War, after the flight of the planters who had built the church, the Negro population took possession of it. It served as a school and a meeting hall as well as a church.

A few months after the end of the war, in July of 1865, it was the setting for outdoor closing exercises of the Penn School which Laura Towne had started in the "Brick Church." The premises were bright with flags, oleander blossoms, and the Sunday best apparel of pupils, parents, and teachers. On this occasion the Reverend Dr. Richard Fuller, former island plantation owner and onetime minister of the Baptist Church of Beaufort, who was well known to the islanders, accompanied Secretary of War Salmon P. Chase on a visit. The audience assembled between the old church and the new quarters of the Penn School which had been sent to the island in prefabricated sections by the Pennsylvania Freedman's Relief Association. Beneath a canopy of oak trees an old man began to sing:

> *"Ma-a-assa Fullah a-sittin' on de*
> *tree ob life,*
> *Ma-a-assa Fullah a-sittin' on de*
> *tree ob life,*
> *Roll, Jordan roll!"*

The whole congregation joined in. The song was then repeated time and time again substituting the names of General Rufus Saxton and Secretary of War Chase for "Ma-a-assa Fullah."

After Dr. Fuller closed the ceremonies with a benediction he was besieged by former slaves who had known him before the "big gun shoot," crowding around him to touch him and remind him of the days when he used to preach to them and of even more distant days when he was a "little 'un," and they used to hunt and fish together.

St. Helena's Baptist Church

Highway 21
St. Helena Island

St. Helena's Baptist Church, completed in 1855, is also referred to as the "Brick Church." It was originally so designated to distinguish it from a nearby Episcopal Chapel of Ease built around 1725 of tabby with a white stucco finish which was known as the "White Church." The

chapel was destroyed by a forest fire in 1886. Its ruins and graveyard may still be seen.

Bricks of a soft pink shading laid in varying patterns give one of the few touches of ornamentation to the stalwart, almost ponderous structure. On the severely plain walls bricks form pilaster type projections, without capitals or shafts, which frame and provide recesses for the windows. The facade has a design of bricks arranged to form a protruding saw-tooth design

The Fripp Plantation
St. Helena Island

The Fripp name, firmly woven into the fabric of the history of St. Helena and neighboring islands, appeared in the Low Country as far back as 1695 when a member of the clan, John Fripp, was awarded Fripp Island by King William III of England for services as a privateer against Spanish ships in the New World. It would appear that this was the same John Fripp who purchased land on Edisto Island in 1707.

The name of the Fripp who built this white frame dwelling on St. Helena around 1800 is not known. At the beginning of the Civil War Edgar W. Fripp had inherited it. As he was a minor Federal troops moved in to "safeguard" the property. At the end of the war he was able to regain 732 acres of his inheritance of 1,284 acres and his ancestral home where he lived until the early 1900's when he sold the house and surrounding acreage for a hunting preserve. preserve.

The house is Adam in style and concept and contains fine woodwork similar to that of the John Mark Verdier House on Beaufort's Bay Street.

From a single lower veranda an entrance door with an elliptical fanlight and rectangular side lights opens into a wide central hall. A gently curving stairway at the back framed by a wide arch and decorated piers leads to two bedrooms upstairs.

To the right of the hall the large drawing room features superlative wood carving and an Adam mantel. On the overmantel there is a mural by an itinerant artist of those distant days whose work still "glows with Tyrian rays." Two large book cases with glass doors framed by ornate cornices and pilasters are beside the mantel. Paneled wainscoting, dentil molding and an alcove in the wall at right angles to the fireplace wall add further finish to the room.

In June of 1969 the house and 830 acres of pastures, pecan orchards and farm land were sold by William C. Anderson who lived in the house for three years and did a great deal of the repair and restoration work himself. Mr. Anderson came to admire and respect the non-rigid peg and beam construction of the house and attributed its remarkable strength and endurance to flexibility under the lash of strong storm winds.

Coffin Point Plantation

The Thomas Aston Coffin House
St. Helena Island
Home of Mr. and Mrs. George C. McMillan

An avenue of oaks half a mile long leading to Coffin Point Plantation draws the expectant gaze of the visitor onward to the "big house" built in the Adam style in the early 1800's by Thomas Aston Coffin. The spacious house is placed on high ground overlooking Port Royal Sound and the Atlantic Ocean on a site which three hundred years earlier might have served as a vantage point for the Indians of St. Helena Island, in "the land called Chicora", to witness the arrival of the first Spanish explorers led by Pedro de Quexos.

The white frame house stands on a high basement and has verandas across the front and rear. Early colonists imported the idea of a piazza from the West Indies, taking a good idea and making it better by building broader ones. The house has center halls with rooms on each side on the second and third story levels and contains notable woodwork with archways framed by graceful fluted posts and intricate rosettes.

The Coffins were prominent leaders of Charleston society, but they lived quietly while in residence at Coffin Point, reserving their mansion in Charleston for elaborate entertainments. During the Civil War Federal officers found in the island home a large library which they confiscated for shipment north.

Mr. Coffin was a highly successful planter of long staple cotton owning more than 2,000 acres of land on the island and 260 slaves. He was a friend of William Elliott who had raised the first successful crop of sea island cotton on Hilton Head Island in 1790 and the two exchanged ideas about production methods. Mr. Coffin's cotton shipments marked with a "pinch-toe" coffin brought top prices in the London market and his fellow Low Country planters counted themselves fortunate when they could obtain his carefully selected cotton seed.

St. Helena Island was the scene of many of the events of the "Port Royal Experiment" which began in March of 1862 as northern missionaries, teachers, and abolitionists arrived in the region on the heels of Federal troops to teach the former slaves reading, writing, morality, and sanitation after the departure of the plantation owners, including Mr. Coffin and his family, (who never returned).

One of the teachers, Miss Harriet Ware, rode horseback among the cabins to teach the Negroes how to bake bread with yeast and wheat flour. She remarked of the house at Coffin Point in 1862, "It was well built in good style originally, but is very old and has been abused. It must have been handsomely furnished to judge from the relics, rosewood tables, sideboards and wash stands with marble tops, sofas that must have been of the best."

Edward Philbrick, engineer and architect from Brookline, Massachusetts, who arrived at the age of thirty-four to work without compensation and even contributed $1,000 toward the "experiment" bought Coffin Point Plantation as well as several other plantations in 1863.

The wife of a later owner, Pennsylvania Senator James Donald Cameron, the young and elegant Elizabeth Sherman Cameron, was a devoted friend and correspondent of Henry Adams. As he ranged the world he wrote Mrs. Cameron of his impressions of people and places. He visited the Camerons in January 1894 and reported, "The comfort is great to escape the dreary collapse of society in the North."

Mr. and Mrs. J. E. McTeer owned the home from 1952 until 1968. It is now the home of Mr. and Mrs. George C. McMillan.

St. Luke's Methodist Church
State Highway 170 near Prichardville

A sign on the front of St. Luke's Methodist Church, "Founded in 1875," tells only part of the story of the long and honorable history of a church which first sheltered an Episcopal congregation. The building was consecrated in 1824 by Bishop Nathaniel Bowen as the second parish church of St. Luke's. It is still referred to occasionally as the Bull Hill Church recalling John Bull of Bull Hill Plantation, who gave four acres of land to the first parish church which was erected in 1786 on a site now marked only by a lonely grave half a mile from the present white frame building. The first structure fell into ruins and probably burned. Land was given by John Guerard for a new church. With the passing of the years other places of worship

replaced the Bull Hill Church and its membership dwindled. In 1875 a newly organized congregation of the Methodist Episcopal Church purchased the building from the Episcopal vestry. For several years afterwards the north side was reserved for Episcopalians. The Methodists have kept the old building repaired and painted and the worship, begun so long ago, continues in these modern times.

In ante bellum days the slave members of the congregation came in by what is now the main entrance of the church to climb narrow stairs to a small gallery supported by eight-sided posts. White worshipers used two doors beside the chancel rostrum. High-backed box pews raised slightly above the original wide planks of the floors are still in use. There are four tall roundheaded, multipaned windows on each side of the building and fan lights over the doorways.

Ruins of Sheldon Episcopal Church
Highway 17 near Gardens Corners

Stately and poignant ruins stand today where once there was "the second best church in the Province, and by many esteem'd a more beautiful building than St. Philip's (of Charleston) . . . beautifully pew'd and ornamented." Thus read a report sent to the Church of England by an official visitor to Sheldon, the parish church of St. William's, twenty-odd years after its completion in 1753.

British troops under the command of General Augustine Prevost marching from Savannah to Charleston in 1780 paused to burn it. Nearly fifty years later it was rebuilt using the old brick walls of three-and-a-half-foot English bond. The story of destruction was repeated in 1865 by the Yankee General, William Tecumseh Sherman, who moved with his torch into South Carolina from Georgia.

The spirit of the old church still lives in the quiet forest, however, and a pilgrimage makes its way to the ruins every spring on the second Sunday after Easter. Commemorative services, sponsored by St. Helena's Church of Beaufort, are held amid the towering columns, semi-circular bastions, durable arches, and crumbling brick walls in a cathedral-like setting of oaks with mourning veils of Spanish moss.

In 1815 the Reverend Christian Hackel conducted a service in the rubble which the British had left. "It was an occasion of rare interest," one of the worshipers chronicled. "The building was in ruins; the walls and columns of the portico alone were standing - sad monument to the violence and lawlessness of those times. The forest had resumed its sway, and the interior was filled with a large growth of trees, which had to be cut down by one of the parishioners. Boards were placed on the stumps for seats, and with no covering but the clear blue sky of a balmy spring day, the man of God proclaimed to a large and respectable audience the glad tidings of salvation."

Huspah Plantation

The George Waterhouse House
Off of Highway 17, Near Sheldon
Home of Mr. and Mrs. Sumner Pingree, Jr.

Not much remains of old habitations in the northern part of the county to mark the influx of pioneers early in the eighteenth century when settlers began to find their way to the rich and productive lands around Huspah Creek. They traded with the Indians, shipped naval stores and planted cotton, indigo, and food crops "to satisfy ye belly . . . as ye foundation of ye Plantation," as admonished by the Lords Proprietors from England. Beyond Huspah Creek in the lands toward the Combahee River

rice culture flourished. But there was also danger. Indian raids and scalping forays were frequent. In 1715 the Yamassees wiped out the trading post at Pocotaligo. During the Revolution the British ravaged the countryside and burned nearby Sheldon Church.

Of the later houses, however, one of the most interesting is a century-old low rambling house sheltered beneath large oaks on the banks of Huspah Creek.

Its story begins with the construction of a white frame house by George Waterhouse, Sr., of Beaufort, soon after the Civil War.

In the early part of the present century a later owner, Felix Ewing, added three rooms and a

small office to the original structure. Mr. Ewing brought pine wainscoting, mantels, doors, beams, cupboards and floor boards from an old tavern in Vermont and reassembled them in rooms carefully built to scale to accomodate the old woodwork.

Mr. and Mrs. Sumner Pingree, Jr. bought the house in 1961 and have added two additional rooms-a large drawing room and a bedroom. The old parts of the house blend with the new, unified by the use of English bricks from an old house in Charleston and antiqued wood paneling. The rooms are furnished with many fine antiques from Europe and with Early American pine and maple furniture. The home was sold in May 1970 to Mrs. C. F. Benedict.

seventy-nine

Delagaye or De Lagaye) and his wife Catherine Gautier, settled on a 250-acre tract of land near Beaufort on the Banks of Battery Creek.

The small tabby house which they built there around 1745 with walls nearly two feet thick survives today with many patchings and mendings, having borne the passing years creditably in its remote, park-like setting. It was restored in 1938 and a wing was added in 1950.

The large chimneys on the east and west sides of the house have contrasting brick of a dark bluish-gray glaze inlaid in an interlocking diamond pattern. Four slender posts support the roof of a brick-floored porch considered to be a later addition. The scored stucco finish of part of the facade to the right of the entrance has worn away, exposing the texture of large oyster shells used in the tabby building material.

Within, the house is intimate and charming, with recessed windows, paneled walls, and a narrow, winding stairway leading to bedrooms on the second floor.

To the east of the house there is a formal garden, added in recent years, with a beguiling old world personality. Two stone owls are posted at the entrance. Back of the surrounding low lacework wall there is, most appropriately, a sundial and a languid fountain surrounded by plantings of azaleas, camellias, pyracantha, and loquat.

The Jean de la Gaye House

Retreat Plantation
Jericho Road off of State Highway 280
Home of Mr. and Mrs. Louis Pinckney

Jean de la Gaye, a Swiss wine merchant, arrived off the South Carolina shores in 1733 bound for the newly established Huguenot and Swiss settlement at Purrysburg in what is now Jasper County, twenty-two miles from the mouth of the Savannah River. The Purrysburg venture,

an ill-starred project under the direction of Colonel Jean Pierre Purry of Neufchatel, Switzerland, and subsidized by the British crown, disappeared in the early 1800's. Many of the colonists found that Purry's "Carolina Paradise" offered only hardship, illness, and death. Some remained in the settlement, which at one time had a hundred houses, to produce hemp, silk, wine, indigo, and cotton. Others moved on. Jean de la Gaye, (sometimes spelled

Honey Horn Plantation

The William J. Graham House
Hilton Head Island
Home of Mr. and Mrs. Fred C. Hack

Honey Horn Plantation is the only survivor of the many plantation homes which flourished on Hilton Head Island, reaching back to the time when it was part of the Barony granted by the Lords Proprietors to Irishman John Bayley of Ballingclough, County of Tipperary, in 1698. The two hundred acres "home place" of Honey Horn, buffered by clumps of trees, pasture lands, and the quiet waters of a tidal stream from the nearby island areas of golf courses, inns, resort homes, and white beaches, stands today as a link with a faraway past.

For many years, Indian uprisings, slave revolts, Spanish incursions, and French threats gave the island the reputation of being a very unsafe place to live. Boats patrolled from Beaufort north to the Stono River and southward past Hilton Head Island, searching the horizon for marauders until 1763 when a treaty with Spain gave England a clear title to Georgia and the Port Royal area.

By 1776 twenty-five families lived on Hilton Head Island. After the War of the Revolution, James Hanahan, a planter from Edisto Island, bought a large tract of land including lots 10 and 11 of Bayley's Barony. (Many believe that through a process of island transmutation "Hanahan Plantation" became "Honey Horn Plantation.")

John and James Stoney acquired the property in 1805 and later sold it to William J. Graham, who began construction of the plantation's spacious one-storied house just before the outbreak of the Civil War.

The Reverend Charles C. Pinckney described the life of those days in an account of his Grandmother Elliott's house at Myrtle Bank Plantation, four miles from Honey Horn, in an address in 1878 before the South Carolina Historical Society:

"I recall an old fashioned country home on the river bank, when the shades of evening and the breath of spring lured the family to the piazza. The harp in hands of a skillful musician, accompanied by her brothers on flute and clarinet, imprinted sweet sounds on the memory . . . Down the broad avenue over-arched by the patriarchal live oaks and verdant magnolia, you saw moonbeams dancing on the waters of Port Royal, the peerless river of our southern coasts, while the orange trees and jasmine embowering the piazza and clambering up its posts perfumed the air with odors sweet . . The Negroes' keen ear for music would draw them from their homes. Seated on the grass around the house, they counted it a privilege to hear Miss Mary's harp."

For action and excitement there were boat racing, fishing, and hunting. Friends came by the boatload from surrounding islands for oyster roasts on the beach.

All came to an end when Union forces took over the island. Homes and fields were destroyed - by burning and plundering Federal soldiers and Negroes and by Confederate raiding parties who slipped through the waterways in small boats to destroy bales of cotton ready for shipment northward, fire the crops still growing in the fields, and burn the homes to prevent use by the enemy. The Grahams were unable to redeem Honey Horn when the war was over. In 1863 Freeman Dodd bought 1,000 acres of Honey Horn Plantation for $200. He sold it three months later for $10,000. For nearly seventy-five years following Dodd's windfall Hilton Head Island slumbered. The plantation was bought and sold several times until it was purchased in 1931 as a hunting preserve by New York investment executives, Langdon K. Thorne and Alfred L. Loomis. They added a wing with a drawing room thirty-six by twenty-four feet and two additional bedrooms which extended the length of the house to 175 feet.

Furniture of walnut adorned with brass *applique'*, marble-topped tables, mahogany tables with dolphin-shaped legs, Italian hand painted accessories, French cane beds, and Piranesi etchings made the long journey from decorators' show rooms on Fifth Avenue to a final crossing by boat to the island.

For a decade the "big house" on Honey Horn Plantation was an exclusive hunting lodge, a retreat for some of the nation's industrialists and other prominent men who came to shoot deer, quail, wild turkeys and ducks.

Mr. and Mrs. Fred C. Hack who have made their home on the island since 1950, moved into the old house in 1965. In its renovation they have retained many of the finer furnishings. Mr. Hack, who had a major role in the rebirth of long-isolated Hilton Head Island and its development into an internationally acclaimed resort community, is a collector of historical artifacts. The squire of Honey Horn has an extensive collection of antique bottles, Indian projectile points, some of which are as old as 9,000 years, and other relics found on Honey Horn Plantation or elsewhere on the island.

Stoney Creek Presbyterian Chapel

McPhersonville, S. C.
Future Location - Hilton Head Island

Beaufort County will soon add another important building to its roster of old churches. The Sea Pines Plantation Company has arranged with the Charleston Presbytery to move the Stoney Creek Presbyterian Chapel from McPhersonville in Hampton County to its new Harbour Town Development on Hilton Head Island and will preserve it as a historic chapel where the waters of Calibogue Sound lap the peaceful island shores.

The last service held in the chapel was on May 26, 1968, to commemorate the 225th anniversary of the organization of the chapel's mother church, the Independent Presbyterian Church of Stoney Creek, a casualty of the War Between the States (it was destroyed by Sherman's troops in 1865). The Independent Presbyterian Church of Stoney Creek was organized in 1743 by settlers of the Indian Land near Pocotaligo fifteen miles from Beaufort. It was reorganized in 1772, chartered in 1785 as the Independent Presbyterian Church of Prince William's Parish and rechartered in 1816. The old church was prosperous in its early years, being supported by a rich congregation drawing its wealth from rice, cotton and indigo plantations. The church owned slaves and hired them out for revenue.

The chapel at McPhersonville was completed in 1833 to serve a large colony of rice planters from the Combahee River and nearby streams who made the little village a summer refuge in the healthful piney woods. It survived the Civil War years as a Federal Hospital and served the shattered remnants of the Congregation after the war. Until 1968 it continued to use the communion cups of the mother church inscribed "For the Presbyterian Meeting" given by Evins Palmer in 1753 and communion plates presented by A. F. Gregorie in 1847.

The first of the long chain of ministers of the Independent Presbyterian Church of Stony Creek was the Reverend William Hutson who wrote its covenant and articles of faith based on the Westminster Confession which declared it to be independent of every other church. Its second minister, the Reverend Archibald Simpson (a scotsman), left in his diary a valuable record of pre-revolutionary society, politics and economics. The church was received into the Charleston Presbytery in 1855 when the Reverend James B. Dunwoody was pastor. The Reverend Mr. Dunwoody performed the marriage ceremony of his cousin, Martha Bullock and Theodore Roosevelt at Roswell, Georgia. They were the parents of President Theodore Roosevelt and the grandparents of President Franklin Delano Roosevelt. Just before the Civil War the minister was the Reverend S. Edward Axon whose daughter Ellen, married Woodrow Wilson.

The rectangular white frame building of the chapel, crowned with a bell tower and spire, has arched windows with green shutters on all sides and a portico on the front with four plain rounded posts supporting its roof. Above the entrance door a small stained glass window of gold, mauve and blue has traceries suggestive of the Gothic compatible with the arches of the windows. The sturdy simplicity which characterizes the exterior is present inside in the simple white paneled pulpit with bands of gold leaf. Old kerosene hanging lamps have been wired for electricity and the Detroit-made Farrand & Votey organ remains in good voice. The chapel is a little gem well worthy of preservation.

It is believed that the church was originally named for Stony Creek but an 'e' has crept into the spelling which associates it with the well known Low Country Stoney family. However, John R. Todd and Francis M. Hutson in *Prince William's Parish and Plantations* points out the fact that the lands around Stony Creek were settled long before the Stoney family arrived in America in 1774. Although George Howe, in his two-volume *History of the Presbyterian Church in South Carolina* uses both spellings, he appears to prefer "Stoney." The 1847 communion plates are inscribed "Stony", but old books and hymnals in the chapel bear the name "Stoney." It would appear that the 'e' in the name is there to stay.

The Card House

Bluffton
Owned by Mrs. Anna C. Hunter

The Card House, popularly regarded as the oldest home in Bluffton, was built around 1825. How it got its name is anybody's guess. This picturesque little river town was originally settled in 1825 as a summertime resort and was favored by Low Country planters and their families. Card-playing was undoubtedly one of the pastimes enjoyed beside the River May, and one of the legends - that the house was won (or lost?) in a card game - may be true.

The property is now owned by the distinguished Savannah author and editor, Mrs. Anna C. Hunter.

The Church of the Cross
Bluffton

The Episcopal Church of the Cross in Bluffton, sheltered in a peaceful tree-shaded setting on the banks of the May River, is an interesting example of rustic Gothic architecture. Built of weathered cypress batten on board upon a foundation of brick, its facade is broken by tall, arched mullioned windows with rose-tinted diamond shaped panes framed by green shutters. Artfully placed medallions with the same pink panes add grace and balance.

Old Blufftonians insist that a French architect, Dimmick (whose first name does not emerge from records at hand), the designer of "Kirk's Folly" on Rose Hill Plantation in the Gothic Revival style, planned the Church of the Cross. However, in *The Charleston News and Courier* of June 27, 1854, a request is printed for "proposals from some competent mechanic" to build The Church of the Cross and it referred the applicant to the Building Committee or to "Col. E. B. White, architect, who submitted the plan and specifications which were accepted by the vestry." Perhaps both Mr. Dimmick and Colonel White contributed ideas to the new church.

Colonel Edwin Baker White was one of Charleston's leading architects. He was partial to the ecclesiastical Gothic style and is credited with its introduction into South Carolina. He was a master of the use of towers, turrets, steeples, and spires. Other examples of his work are Grace Church of Charleston and Trinity Church in Columbia. He also designed the steeple of St. Philip's Church in Charleston, added in 1847 and to this day a landmark of that city.

The church in Bluffton was completed in 1857 at a cost of $5,000 and was consecrated on July 19. The ceremonies marking the event lasted three days with six clergymen, including a Bishop, taking part.

The church is filled with soft light filtered through Spanish moss on the trees outside and reflected from pink interior walls of scored stucco. The strength, simplicity and honesty of its structure is revealed in exposed heavy wooden cross beams which support the roof.

Carved wooden balustrades of galleries built for slaves repeat on both sides of the building the graceful arch motif of the windows. The chancel was remodeled in 1872. The present communion table, lectern, and prayer desk were built in that year from aged walnut of an older pulpit and desk. Ancient closed pews provide seats for the congregation.

A storm in 1898 caused such serious damage that a distressed visitor reported that as he stood in the chancel and looked down the nave, "the clear blue sky was fully exposed to the view through the shattered roof and the crushed end of the church." The nave was reconstructed and a chapel was built into the east end of the church. The chapel is now furnished with hand-hewn pews, pulpit and an old altar brought from St. Edmund's Church of Hardeeville when it was torn down around 1950.

The Church of the Cross is no stranger to violence. A company of Union soldiers came over from Hilton Head Island in 1861 early in the days of the Civil War to loot and plunder Bluffton. They burned much of the village and started to destroy the church, tearing up the organ, throwing its pipes into the May River, and pulling down the pulpit. They were interrupted by a small band of Confederates with an oversized Rebel yell and left hurriedly.

The church's bell was sent to Charleston in 1861 destined for England to be melted down for bullets, but missed the boat. Discovered some ten years later hanging in Porter Military Academy in Charleston, it was returned to its rightful place and in 1898 installed in the belfry which houses it today.

Rose Hill Plantation

The John Kirk House
Near Bluffton
Home of Mr. and Mrs. John Sturgeon

Located in the Okatie section of Beaufort County near Bluffton, Rose Hill Plantation today is one of the most cherished homes in the southeastern section of the United States. Curiously enough, it stood for more than ninety years gaunt and half-completed, hidden in the woods and for long periods abandoned to the elements, known only to animal prowlers and passing huntsmen. So stoutly was it constructed in the beginning that it not only survived, but at times provided shelter for various families. The roof was sound, and the impressive spell of its beauty is credited with saving it from destruction during the Civil War when a Union officer, who was ordered to burn

it, looked it over admiringly and decided against setting it afire.

The house was begun in the late 1850's by Dr. John Kirk on plantation lands dating from a barony - Colleton's Neck or Devil's Elbow Barony - granted Sir John Colleton, grandson of the original Lord Proprietor of the same name by a patent dated December 5, 1718. The new house was referred to around the countryside as "Kirk's Folly." Folly it may have been, but it was magnificently planned, being designed as a splendid formal house in the Gothic Revival style so favored by Queen Victoria. Construction stopped abruptly in 1861 when the War Between the States began, and the workmen walked away leaving a litter of tools and paint pots. The scaffolding was still in place when it was purchased by John Sturgeon in 1946.

Mr. Dimmick, the same French architect associated with the Church of the Cross in nearby Bluffton, is credited with the design of the house. At the entrance, wide steps lead up to a vaulted porch with slender pillars, arches, and wrought iron scrollwork. The windows on the second story repeat the taper of the arches.

Within the baronial entrance hall a free hanging stairway of teak, walnut, and oak of pegged construction flows upward to a gallery from which the bedrooms open. Above, fifty-four feet from the floor, a dome rises and from it two Bacarrat chandeliers are suspended, garlanded with flashing crystals and joined by a fourteen-foot glass shaft. Massive hand carved doors and a Hepplewhite settee curve with the sweep of the rounded rear walls of the hall.

Interior decoration by the late Rogers McClelland is spirited and fittingly elegant for a house created in the grand manner. Throughout there are exquisite details such as Dorothy Doughty Royal Doulton porcelain birds, Royal Crown Derby china, and a needlepoint rug in the hall with amarylis, calla lilies, and

apple blossoms worked into squares with bands of green between against a darker green background. The painstaking restoration included the installation of authentic flooring from an old house in Washington, Georgia, and the services of an artisan brought from New York to hang and restore the dining room wallpaper.

In the drawing room to the left of the great hall stands a white marble Adam mantel with columns of rose peche. "A Portrait of Mrs. Greaves" by Romney, hanging over the mantel, looks serenely over the lovely room. The door to an adjoining solarium is flanked by a pair of Griffon consoles of water gild.

The windows of the solarium frame a view of the surrounding woods and fields which comprise part of the 18,000-acre working plantation, and admit a flood of light to enliven a chandelier of glass day lilies with brass stamens, leaves, and tendrils.

The dining room has its own handsome chandelier. Large and elaborate, it is early Louis XV with the original wood-polished crystal bobeches. Wallpaper with a historic flavor - it was discovered in an old palace in the Piedmont section of Italy - covers the walls. Made in China for demanding English and French tastes of the day, its design is intricate with medallions, tassels, arches, and garlands characteristic of the Louis XVI style.

Across the hall from the drawing room an intimate library provides from a large bay window yet another view of Rose Hill's magnificent surroundings. This room is warm and inviting with eighteenth-century floral wallpaper, a Directoire chandelier, curtains and upholstery of red silk antique moire, and a game table flanked by upholstered Chippendale chairs. The fireplace is framed by a Chippendale mantel. Matching cabinet fronts form casings for book cases on either side and above the fireplace there is a glorious gilt rococo mirror of the same period.

Old Homes & Churches of Beaufort County, South Carolina
BIBLIOGRAPHY

Adams, Henry. *Letters* 1858-1918. Edited by Worthington Chauncey Ford. Boston, Houghton Mifflin, 1930-1938 2 Columes.

Andrews, Beatrice E. *The Catholic Church and the Houses on New Street and Vicinity.* A paper for the Beaufort County Historical Society, 1966.

Betts, Albert Deems. *History of South Carolina Methodism.* Columbia Advocate Press, 1952

Danner, Howard E. *Beaufort in the Civil War.* A paper for the Beaufort County Historical Society, 1960.

Fickling, Evan Edwards. *Eight Beaufort Homes.* A paper for the Beaufort County Historical Society, 1965.

Fripp, Nellie. *Bluffton and the Okatee.* A paper for the Beaufort County Hisotrical Society, 1951.

Graydon, Nell S. *Tales of Beaufort.* Beaufort. The Beaufort Book Shop, 1964.

Grayson, William John. *Autobiography* 1788-1863. Copy in Beaufort County Library of Original Manuscript in Possession of the South Caroliniana Library, Columbia, S. C.

Hardy, John W. *Prince William's Parish.* A paper for the Beaufort County Historical Society, 1961.

Hardy, Susan Martin. *Old Houses on the Bluff.* A paper for the Beaufort County Historical Society, 1965.

Holmgren, Virginia C. *Hilton Head: A Sea Island Chronicle.* Hilton Head Island, Hilton Head Island Publishing Company, 1959.

Howe, George. *History of the Presbyterian Church in South Carolina.* Volumes I and II. © 1965 and 1966 by Synod of South Carolina, Presbyterian Church in the United States. Lithographed by State Printing Company, Columbia, S. C.

Inglesby, Edith. *A Corner of Carolina.* Columbia, S. C. The State Printing Company, 1968.

Johnson, Guion Griffis, *Social History of the Sea Islands.* Chapel Hill, University of North Carolina Press, 1930.

Johnson, John Archibald. *Beaufort and the Sea Islands.* Beaufort Republican, 1873.

Jones, Katherine M. *Port Royal Under Six Flags.* Indianapolis-New York. The Bobbs-Merrill Company, Inc., 1950.

King, Joe M. *A History of South Carolina Baptists.* General Board of the South Carolina Baptist Convention, 1964.

Lengnick, Lena Wood. *Beaufort Memoirs.* Copy in the Beaufort County Library, 1936. (Revised for Women's Society of Christian Service, Carteret Street Methodist Church, Beaufort, 1961).

Milling, Chapman J. *Exile Without an End.* Columbia, S. C. Bostick & Thornley, Inc., 1943.

Perry, Grace Fox. *Moving Finger of Jasper.* Jasper County Confederate Centennial Commission, no date.

Ravenal, Beatrice St. Julien. *Architects of Charleston.* Charleston, S. C., Carolina Art Association, 1954.

Rose, Willie Lee. *Rehearsal for Reconstruction.* Indianapolis, The Robbs Merrill Company, Inc. 1964.

Runnette, Mabel. *Early Settlement of Beaufort Town - 1700-1725.* A paper for the Beaufort County Historical Society, 1943.

Sterling, Dorothy. *Captain of the Planter.* Garden City, N. Y. Double-day & Company, Inc., 1958.

Theus, Nita Grimsley. *Catholicity in Beaufort - St. Peter's Catholic Church.* A paper in the Beaufort County Library, 1936.

Theus, Nita Grimsley. *Presbyterian Faith and Churches in Beaufort, South Carolina.* A paper in the Beaufort County Library, 1938.

Thomas, Albert Sidney. *The Episcopal Church in South Carolina - 1820-1957.* Columbia, S. C., Printed by the R. L. Bryan Company, 1957.

Todd, John R. and Hutson, Francis M. *Prince William's Parish and Plantations.* Richmond, Virginia. Garrett & Massie, 1935.